D1031414

Acknowledgements:
The publishers wish to thank everybody who assisted in collecting the information and photographs contained in this book, particularly Caroline Popovic, Nancy Atkinson and Chris Huxley. Around the island there were many other people and organisations who gave their time and advice. We would especially like to thank Alan Hunter, at the Royal St. Lucian Hotel, his charming wife Jane and his delightful team of staff. Thanks also go to MRI International in London; Peter and Beverly Hughes for their hospitality and kindness; Magnus Alnabeck at the Ladera Resort; Nicky Roberts; Sarah Carpenter; the St. Lucia Tourism Board, in particular Fenna Williams and Hilary Modeste and finally, to the people of St. Lucia for making our work on this guide such a delight.

First published by:
Cadogan Books plc,
London House, Parkgate Road, London, SW11 4NQ, United Kingdom

In the USA by:
The Globe Pequot Press
PO Box 480, Guilford, Connecticut 06437-0888, United States of America

Distributed in St. Lucia by:
Island Connection Limited, PO Box GM 828, Castries, St. Lucia. Telephone: (758) 450-9418; Fax: (758) 452-7923/450-9417

ISBN: 0-7627-0595-7
A catalogue record for this book is available from the British Library
Library of congress Cataloging-in-Publication data is available

Copyright © Indigo Books Limited 2000
Photographs by: Duncan Willetts and Debbie Gaiger, except for pages Chris Huxley (pages 110, 117, 142 (bottom), 143, 135); Anse Chastanet (pages 126); Mike Seale (pages 73, 74, 75, 76, 77 (top), 78, 79 (bottom), 80, 81, 82).

Designed by: RB Graphics, "Rickettswood", Norwood Hill, Horley, Surrey RH6 0ET United Kingdom.
Editors: Barbara Balletto and Debbie Gaiger
Proof-reading: Liz Sutherland

Printed and bound in China by Jade Productions

indigo guide to st lucia

The Globe Pequot Press

CADOGAN
island guides

Guilford, Connecticut   London, England

ents

A look at the island's
finest beaches.

The waters around St. Lucia are
a perfect place to enjoy a yacht
charter, catamaran day trip or a
sunset cruise.

Nowhere is the rich diversity of
nature displayed to such
magnificent effect as on the
coral reef of St. Lucia.

St. Lucia is home to many
fabulous floral species imported
from around the world.

Castries

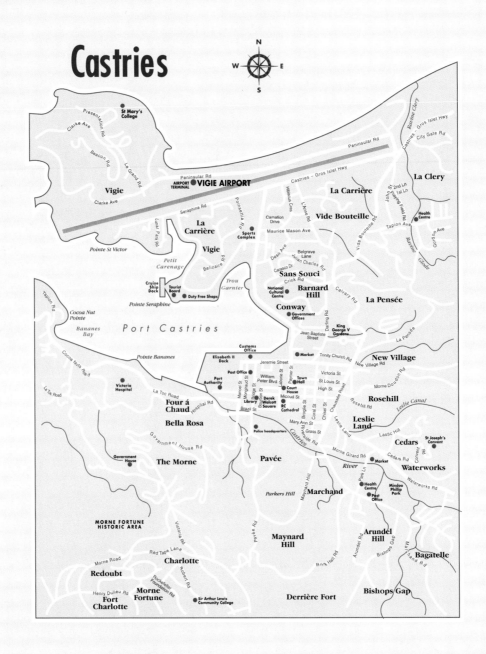

N W E S

St Mary's College
Presentation Rd
Clarke Ave
Beacon Rd
La Grand Rd

Vigie

Clarke Ave

Pointe St Victor

Peninsular Rd

Peninsular Rd
AIRPORT TERMINAL **VIGIE AIRPORT**

Castries – Gros Islet Hwy

Castries – Gros Islet Hwy
Rastner Clery
City Gate Rd

La Clery

John St 2nd Ln
1st Ln
Playing Field Rd

La Carrière

Hibiscus Ave
L'Anse Rd

Vide Bouteille

Vide Bouteille Rd

Tapion Ave
Rastner
Gade

Gordon Ave

Health Centre

Seraphine Rd

La Carrière

Lucas Park Rd

Sports Complex

Carnation Drive

Maurice Mason Ave

Carasco Dr

Desir Ave
Belgrave Lane
Julian Charles Rd

Vigie

Belizaire Rd
Poinsettia Rd

Petit Carenage

Trou Garnier

Sans Souci

Crick Rd

National Cultural Centre

Barnard Hill

Calvary Rd

La Pensée

Cruise Ship Dock
Tourist Board
Duty Free Shops

Pointe Seraphine

Conway

Government Offices

Jean Baptiste Street

Darling Rd

King George V Gardens

La Pensée

Cocoa Nut Pointe

Bananes Bay

Port Castries

Pointe Bananes

Customs Office

Elizabeth II Dock

Market

Trinity Church Rd

New Village Rd

New Village

Tapion Rd

Cocoa Nuts Road

Port Authority

Post Office

Jeremie Street

Palmer St

Victoria St

Morne Dudon Rd

La Toc Road

La Toc Road

Victoria Hospital

Manoel St
Mongiraud St
Brazil St
Bridge St
Coral St
Library

William Peter Blvd

Town Hall

Court House
Micoud St
Derek Walcott Square
RC Cathedral

St Louis St
High St

Brazil St

Mary Ann St

Broglie St
Coral St
Chisel St

Grass St

Chaussee Road

Rosehill

Rosehill Rd

Leslie Land

Lastic Hill

Leslie Canal

Four á Chaud

Bella Rosa

Government House Rd

Hospital Rd

Police headquarters

Castries River

Leslie Lane

Convent Rd

St Joseph's Convent

Cedars

Cedars Rd

Waterworks

Government House

The Morne

Pavée

Morne Girard Rd

River

Market

Mindoo Phillip Park

Waterworks Rd

MORNE FORTUNE HISTORIC AREA

Parkers Hill

Maynard Hill

Marchand

Park Ln

Health Centre

Post Office

Arundel Hill

Arundel Rd

Bishops Gap

Mahand Rd

Bagatelle

Morne Road

Red Tape Lane

Charlotte

Victoria Rd

Robert Rd

Pavée Rd

Maynard Hill

Rock Hall Rd

Bishops Gap

Mahand Rd

Redoubt

Henry Dulieu Rd

Fort Charlotte

Morne Fortune

Rockefeller Foundation Rd

Sir Arthur Lewis Community College

Derrière Fort

Bishops Gap

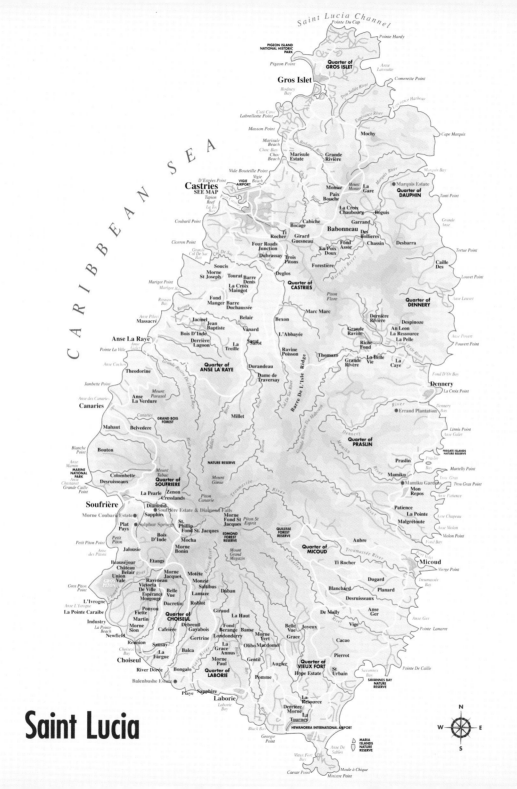

Saint Lucia

essential lists

lively places to get uncorked ...

- The Lime
- Snooty Agouti
- Spinnaker's
- The Eagles' Inn
- The Three Amigos
- Snamrock's
- Indies
- Rain Restaurant
- The Hummingbird Bar
- The Triangle Pub

great buys ...

- Zaka Masks
- Fine art by the island's best artists
- Tapes or CDs of local musicians
- Colourful local t-shirts
- Local pottery
- Hand-made crafts, including jewellery
- Caribbean Perfume
- Dazzling batiks by Caribelle Batik
- Silk screen prints by Bagshaws

lively places to eat ...

- Key Largo
- Mariner's Restaurant
- Razmataz
- Memories of Hong Kong
- Capone's – La Piazza
- La Panache at Henry's
- Doolittle's at Marigot Bay
- The Bistro

great places to visit ...

- Pigeon Island National Park
- The Marquis Estate
- La Sikwi Estate
- The Sulphur Springs
- The Soufrière Estate and Diamond Falls
- Morne Coubaril
- Fregate Island
- The Maria Islands
- Mamiku Gardens
- Errand Plantation
- Balembouche Estate

fabulous places to eat if money's no object ...

- L'Epicure at the Royal St. Lucian
- The Oriental at the Rex St. Lucian
- The Plantation at Jalousie
- Dasheene at Ladera
- Froggie Jack's
- The Coal Pot
- Capone's
- The Great House
- Bon Appetit

great beaches ...

- Reduit Beach
- Vigie Beach
- Anse Chastanet
- Anse L'Ivrogne
- Anse de Sable
- Grand Anse
- Comerette Point
- Cas en bas
- Anse Cochon
- Jalousie Beach

great experiences ...

- A sunset cruise aboard the *Brig Unicorn*
- A day cruise on *Endless Summer* to Soufrière and Marigot Bay
- Snorkel in Anse Cochon or the waters around Anse Chastanet
- Horseback ride along deserted beaches on the east coast
- Join a hike through the magnificent rainforest
- Parasail above the beaches
- Visit the Friday night fish-fry at Anse La Raye on the west coast
- Take a trip on St. Lucia Helicopters for a bird's-eye view of the island
- Watch the sun set between the Pitons from the Ladera Resort
- Hike to the top of Gros Piton
- Scuba dive amidst some of the finest reefs in the Caribbean

.....the

saint lucia experience

Sixty million years ago Nature laid on a spectacular show. It was an extravaganza of epic proportions with a kaleidoscopic refulgence of fiery explosions seldom seen since. When the dust and debris had settled the result of this upheaval was revealed – a dazzling jewel of an island shimmering in the azure blue of the Caribbean Sea.

This turbulent birth has left St Lucia with a fascinating natural legacy. The island is almost entirely volcanic with some of the oldest rock formations found at the extreme northern and southern tips of the island.

More recently, between thirty to forty million years ago, an extended sequence of volcanic activity filled in the *Barre de l'Isle* – literally the "barrier of the island", a ridge of hills that separates the

Photographs clockwise from left: the walls of Anse Chastanet are decorated with fabulous paintings by artists from all over the world; Smuggler's Cove on the north-west coast; delicate crimson orchid; golden sunset over the west coast.

windward and leeward sides of St. Lucia – and the rocks underlying the east coast from Grand Anse to the upper Savannes Bay.

However, it is in Soufrière, on the south-west coast, where Mother Nature orchestrated her wildest performance. Here, the main geological structure is a massive, circular depression about 4 miles (6 km) in diameter called the Qualibou Caldera. This enormous, defunct volcanic crater was produced either by a major eruption, or the collapse of a large volcanic cone.

There is evidence of thirty-three consecutive eruptions in this area with as many as 1,000 years elapsing between each one. These violent explosions carried pumice, ash and pyroclastic ejecta as far as 8 miles (13 km) beyond the volcano's rim.

The caldera then collapsed and set the stage for the emergence of large domes and vast volcanic craters. It was at this moment

that the majestic Pitons were formed.

When the volcanic activity stopped and the island cooled, the barren rock underwent a weathering process that produced a primitive type of soil.

As the first seeds, brought by the wind or through bird propagation, germinated in the virgin St. Lucian soil, the subsequent growth cycle began to enrich the earth.

Left: Petit Piton is a fantastic sight when first seen through dense tropical forest on the road to Soufrière. Above: The fabulous St. Lucia parrot. Below: Local folk take a dip in the sparkling waterfall in La Raye River.

Ironically, much of St. Lucia's lush vegetation belies its acid, heavily leached and mineral-deficient soil, especially along the central ridges where top soil is shallow and vulnerable to erosion. These high points are covered with elfin woodland; gnarled, moss-draped trees, deformed by the winds and festooned with epiphytes.

The central rainforest area, about 18,000 acres in all, is dominated by three giant tree species – the chataigner, gommier and mahoe. This is the home of the St. Lucia parrot and the source of many of the island's rivers.

In the lower forest zone that encompass the coastal areas and mangroves, other trees including the balata, laurier, corosol and paletuvier predominate. There are 151 tree species in St. Lucia with thirty-five endemic varieties.

The best soils are found in alluvial deposits along the lower reaches of river valleys such as Roseau,

Photographs clockwise from top left: lone yacht at sunset; colourful rum shop in Anse La Raye; the exotic "bird of paradise" grows throughout St. Lucia; the best way to cool down after a rainforest hike!; the vibrant 'I Love You' bus transports visitors to the Morne Coubaril estate in Soufrière; the black sands at Anse Chastanet are home to the Scuba St. Lucia dive operation; Daniel Jean-Baptitse works on a colourful silkscreen at his studio in the Cap Estate. Right: Fisherman at sunset.

Cul de Sac, Mabouya and the Vieux Fort plain.

The forest zones contain an abundant supply of water which is hardly surprising as the island's annual rainfall is some thirty-five billion gallons. However, most of this ends up in the sea, for the impervious volcanic bedrock offers little in the way of storage and retentive facilities.

By the time the first settlers arrived in St. Lucia the 238 square miles were lush, green and densely forested with plenty of fresh water to drink and abundant wildlife to hunt.

The First People

St. Lucia was first occupied by an Amerindian, pre-ceramic people called the Ciboneys. They were hunters and gatherers who consumed whatever nature provided. They left small trace of their presence and little is known about their time on the island.

They were followed by an Arawakian-speaking people known as the Igneri (many call them simply, the Arawaks). They

were adept potters, weavers, builders, agriculturists and shipwrights. By 200 AD, these industrious people were established throughout the Windward Island chain. The Igneri enjoyed nearly 800 years of peace before they were overcome by a new tribe. The Kalinago, better known as the Carib Indians (a derogatory and untrue label conceived by Europeans to signify that these people were cannibals) were warriors by nature. They were master mariners and fishermen and had little time for cultivation. They quickly dominated the pastoral Igneri, doing away with the males and intermarrying with the women. The two sexes even spoke different languages.

When the sail of the first European ship was sighted on the horizon, the Kalinago were supreme rulers of the Windward Islands. They called St. Lucia *Iouanaloa* (meaning "where the iguana is found"). Some of the early explorers, the Spanish, gave them a wide berth. They

15

preferred to deal with the Tainos, a peaceful tribe, related to the Igneris who occupied the northern Antilles, rather than take on the Kalinago. More to the point, they found no gold in the Windward Islands. In 1499, Juan de la Cosa the map-maker who worked with Christopher Columbus, became the first European to chart St. Lucia. He called the island *El Falcon*. To this day, the origins of the name Saint Lucia remain a rungular conundrum.

In 1550, the French privateer, François de Clerc better known to his friends as *Jambe de Bois* (or wooden leg), made St. Lucia's Pigeon Island his secret head-quarters and anchored a fleet of warships. From this base it is believed that he captured at least four Spanish galleons. But he does not seem to have disturbed the Kalinago.

There is one mention of European interaction with the Kalinago. It appears in the *Primrose Journal*, a ship's record kept by Martin Frobisher, vice-admiral in Sir Francis Drake's expedition of

Top: Part of the Black Madonna *by local artist Dunstan St. Omer. The painting can be found in the village of Jackmel. Centre: The historic site of Pigeon Island National Park. Below: The Old Courthouse in Soufrière is now a restaurant.*

1585. The Indians' boats, he remarked were "made like a hogges trowghe, all of one tree."

Despite their murderous and cannibalistic reputation, the Kalinago did trade with the Europeans — at least in the beginning. Distrust and eventual betrayal, especially over land sovereignty, seems to have ruined any hope of peaceful co-existence.

One of the most torrid accounts of a disastrous encounter with St. Lucia's Kalinago was published in 1605 and circulated in London. It carried the immensely long title of *An Houre Glasse of Indian Newes, or A True and Tragicall Discourse, Shewing the most Lamentable Miseries and distressed Calamities Indured by 67 Englishmen, which were Sent for a Supply to the Planting in Guiana in the Years. 1605. Who not Finding the Saide Place, were for Want of Victuall, Left Ashore in Saint Lucia, an Islan of Caniballs, or Men-Eaters in the West Indyes, under the Conduct of Captain Sen-Johns, of all which Said Number, only a 22. are Supposed to be still Living, whereof 4, are lately Returnd into England. Written by John Nicholl, one of the Aforesaid Company.*

Nicholl and his compatriots were bound for Guyana when their vessel, the *Olive Branch*, was blown off course. They eventually landed in St. Lucia and being too weak to continue their journey, Nicholl and his group were deposited ashore to fend for themselves while the boat continued her journey south.

Nicholl tells of meetings with two Kalinago chiefs, Anthonio and his brother, Angrauemart. At first all seemed well; the Kalinago sold the Englishmen thatched huts and traded with them for food supplies such as "Potatoes, Penas (pineapple), Pumpins (pumpkin), Callobashoes (calabash), Guiavas (guava), Tobacco, Turtles, Hens, Chickens, Woodcocks and Cassada".

Another account written by one William Turner – an individual who stayed on the *Olive Branch* – claims that St. Lucia contained "Tygars, Alagartos and other Beasts", although he never verified this information.

The stranded Englishmen remained wary of the Kalinago.

Nicholl records that his party had "mounted our great Peece (cannon) upon broade Tables, which wee our selves had sawne, least the Carrebyes should at any time assault us."

This distrust did not prevent several of Nicholl's party leaving with a group of Kalinago, in search of riches. The Englishmen had seen members of the Kalinago wearing pieces of gold body jewellery and some tribesmen agreed to take the British to the source of the gold. The party never returned and hostilities broke out between the remaining British and the Kalinago.

A subsequent ambush wiped out all but a few Englishmen. The Kalinago then helped the eleven survivors to escape. These survivors traded every last hatchet, knife, bead, shovel and spade in return for a canoe and some cloth for a sail. At one o'clock in the morning on 16 September 1605, the unhappy band escaped: "our Roapes for our Sayle were our Garters."

The Kalinago had little use for what the Europeans held sacred. They were not interested in Christianity and were unmoved by the western passion for gold. They did not believe in organised plantations and, having dominated the region for so long, were in no mood to surrender their territorial imperative.

But they were not to be left in peace. The Windward Islands were rich prizes where exotic produce could be cultivated for export. And, more importantly, they could be held as powerful bargaining instruments in negotiations between warring European factions.

The Kalinago resisted interference for a further half century before the inevitable happened. In 1639, Captain Judlee, an English planter from St. Kitts sponsored a colonisation scheme to St. Lucia. This first venture into occupation ended in disaster for, within a year and a half, everyone was wiped out by the Kalinago.

By 1642, the King of France ceded sovereignty of St. Lucia to the French West Indies Company. Nine years later, St. Lucia was sold to Monsieur du Parquet, Governor of Martinique, and Monsieur Houel for £1,660.

Du Parquet built the first fort in St. Lucia under the command of his agent Rousselau who took the precaution of marrying a Kalinago woman. He lived peacefully until his death in 1655. Then all hell broke loose and of the seven subsequent governors, three were killed by the Kalinago.

After a further nine years of intransigence and unrest, the King of France revoked all grants given to the French West Indies Company. Colonisation attempts, he felt, was too costly in both time and lives. But time was running out for the Kalinago. Faced with ever-increasing pressures of occupation, they finally negotiated a peace treaty with the French and English

agreeing to abandon all rights to the lesser Antilles and to settle only on Dominica and St. Vincent. Their final expulsion from St. Lucia took place in 1663.

Today, the last remaining Kalinago are found at La Pointe Caraîbe, just north of Choiseul on the south-west coast. It is the only place in St. Lucia to still carry its Carib name. Many of the inhabitants bear the Mongoloid features and light-skin of these Amerindian settlers. The ancient art of canoe making is practised in this settlement, as well as pottery and basketry, two other artisanal skills perfected by the wives of ancient warriors.

With the Kalinago out of the picture, the French and the English then set upon each other.

Two Hundred Years of Conflict

The first French influence on St. Lucia was in 1627 when Pierre Belain d'Esnambuc took possession of the island in the name of the French Company of the Isles of Americas. For the next 150 years, despite changing hands fourteen times, St. Lucia

remained predominantly French. During this time, British occupation totalled less than twelve years.

Soufrière was the first town to be established by decree of the French King in 1746. By 1780, twelve towns had been founded. The first road, the *Chemin Royal* was built between 1763 and 1768 and reconstructed in 1787 under the supervision of Lefort de la Tour, the man who carried out the first survey of St. Lucia.

Early crops were indigo, coffee, tobacco and cassava. Unlike other Caribbean islands, sugar did not emerge as an important cash crop in St. Lucia. This was due to constant warfare and natural disasters such as two devastating hurricanes, an earthquake and a yellow fever epidemic.

Above and below: St. Lucia is full of vibrant colour and warmth which is demonstrated in many forms throughout the island.

Anglo-Franco warfare took place at the height of the slave trade (the first slaves arrived in the Caribbean as early as 1511), and St. Lucia, a key pawn in these battles, remained uncolonised until as late as 1641.

The first sugar fields were cultivated in Vieux Fort in 1765. By 1786 there were fifty estates on the island with thirty-two water mills, eighteen cattle mills and three windmills.

Above: Colourful masks by Zaka Masks and Totems are carved from pieces of ancient driftwood. Left: Nutmeg is one of the many spices grown in the Errand Plantation. Centre: Bird's eye view of the verdant interior of St. Lucia. Right: Moonlight shimmers on the waters of the west coast.

By 1843, that number had increased to eighty-three sugar estates, fifty-one water mills, twenty-six cattle mills, six wind-mills and fourteen steam engines. But sugar was unprofitable, and as early as 1870, diversification attempts were made with the introduction of coconuts as an alternative crop.

A census carried out in 1776 shows that St. Lucia's population stood at 2,300 whites, 1,050 mulattos and 16,000 slaves. The agricultural investment totalled one million coffee trees, 300,000 cocoa trees, 1,100 houses and mills, 2,000 cattle, 4,000 sheep, 5,000 acres of cane and 2,000 acres of cotton.

As impressive as it may sound, this was way below the island's capacity. It is estimated that St.

Lucia could have accommodated twice as many people and doubled its production. But ceaseless conflicts meant that many plantations were abandoned. In 1787, Lefort de la Tour recorded that 140 estates had been deserted.

It was a difficult business owning a plantation in St. Lucia. Proprietors had to be ready to flee at a moment's notice depending on the victorious flag of the invading forces. Planting, for the most part, was carried out by marginals, content to put up with insecure land tenure. Labour shortages and perpetual war meant that St. Lucia missed out on much of the sugar boom.

But the colonial powers did not seem to mind St. Lucia's low profitability. They still fought to

control the island for its strategic importance and in various truce agreements between the French and the British, the island was declared a neutral territory as the only workable compromise.

In 1782, when British Admiral Rodney stationed his naval headquarters at Pigeon Island, he urged his government to retain St. Lucia. He said the island was even more valuable than Martinique, not for agricultural but for her harbours and easy access to the rest of the Caribbean.

St. Lucia possesses some of the safest harbours in the West Indies with Cul de Sac, Castries, Choc and Gros Islet all easily defended from the forts at Pigeon Island, the Morne and Vigie. The island was also centrally located and could easily respond to a call to arms elsewhere in the region.

As if to prove his point, the admiral launched one of his most decisive attacks on the French from Pigeon Island. On 8 April 1782, Rodney watched Admiral de Grasse set sail from Martinique with the pride of the French fleet to launch a major attack on Jamaica. He did not waste a second; with Sir Samuel Hood leading and Admiral Drake bringing up the rear, Rodney engaged the French on the 12th April 1782, near the Islands of the Saints, north of Dominica.

The Battle of the Saints was one of the most decisive British naval victories against the French. The French readily appreciated St. Lucia's strategic value and Lefort de la Tour wrote in 1789 that "not one sloop can leave the port of Fort Royal of St. Pierre in Martinique without being visible from the lookout at Pigeon Island."

One historic upheaval to shake St. Lucia was the French Revolution. In 1789 St. Lucia was already experiencing a period of great unrest among the slave population. Out of the 18,000 slaves on the island, some 5,000 or thirty per cent were recent arrivals. History has shown that the most rebellious were those freshly brought in from Africa. By the time the effects of the French Revolution were being felt in St. Lucia around 1791, the island was ripe for rebellion.

Victor Hughes, the black Robespierre of the Isles, brought the revolutionary message to St. Lucia through his trusted lieutenant, Commissaire Goyrand. Under Revolutionary laws, slavery was abolished and the political equality of the coloured man was recognised. The first decree of the abolition of slavery was recorded in St. Lucia on 4 February 1794.

Left: Dazzling frangipani in Mamiku Gardens. Below: Graceful sea fans and myriad corals abound in the underwater world of St. Lucia.

The slave population went wild and proceeded to wipe out the plantation infrastructure. The destruction was orchestrated by the Maroons, the name given to renegade slaves who, prior to the revolution, lived in secret hideouts in the more inaccessible parts of the island. When the revolution arrived, the Maroons joined forces with the French revolutionary army to form the L'Armèe des Bois.

Parish registers were destroyed in Laborie, Choiseul and Anse La Raye. Between 1789 and 1810, St. Lucia lost over 4,000 of her inhabitants which accounted for twenty per cent of the entire population. They had either been killed or had deserted the island.

Many of St. Lucia's valuable documents and records have been irretrievably lost over the years. Castries experienced four disastrous fires in 1796, 1813, 1927 and 1948. As a result,

Above: The sun paints a golden farewell to a memorable day at sea.

much of the original architecture and valuable accounts of the past are lost forever.

In 1795, a guillotine was erected in the Soufrière Square, where Sir Auguste Jean de Sauzay and Gilles Duchaumont both lost their heads. Under the Revolutionary regime, St. Lucia became Ste. Lucie La Fidèle and all the towns were renamed.

Castries, named after Charles, Marquis de Castries, Maréchal of France, became Félicitéville. Dennery, which took its name from the Comte d'Ennery, Governor General of the French Windward Islands in 1768, became Le Republicain. Choiseul, after the Duc de Choiseul, the French Minister of Foreign Affairs, was known as Le Tricolore. Praslin, named in honour of the Duc de Praslin, Ministre de la Marine, was transformed into La Constitution. Micoud, that had taken its name from M. de Micoud, Governor of St. Lucia, became L'Union. Anse La Raye, named after a species of ray that used to frequent the bay, became L'Egalitè. Vieux Fort became La Loi, while Laborie, originally named in honour of the Baron de Laborie, became La Patriote. It was Baron de Laborie

who had first analysed Soufrière's volcanic waters and found that they compared favourably with the mineral springs of Aix-les-Bains in France. He then built the Soufrière mineral baths in 1785. He also constructed new roads and imported varieties of spice from Cayenne to be cultivated in St. Lucia.

Gros Islet was called La Revolution and Soufrière became La Convention. True to revolutionary fervor, what is now the Derek Walcott Square in central Castries, used to be known as Place d'Armes. The Revolutionary government held St. Lucia for fifteen months. L'Armée des Bois, under the command of Commissaire Goyrand, was a force of some 2,000 well-disciplined black soldiers who held off British attempts to retake the island. But information about individual members of St. Lucia's Maroons is sketchy. Flore Bois Gaillard was the female leader of one group. Her headquarters were in Fond Gens Libre (meaning the place of free people) in Soufrière. Marin Padre, a St. Lucian mulatto, led rebel Maroon units in St. Lucia and St. Vincent.

In 1796, Lieutenant-General Sir Ralph Abercrombie, with great difficulty, finally retook St. Lucia for the British. The Maroons eventually laid down their arms in 1797. They refused to submit to slavery that had been reinstated by the British so the authorities formed them into a regiment and shipped them out to Africa.

An Island Identity

St. Lucia changed hands for the last time in 1814. The Treaty of Paris, signed between the British and the French, finally ceded the island to the British. In 1815, St. Lucia became a colony under the British Crown.

While slavery was abolished on 1 August 1834, this initial decree did not mean full liberation. A period of apprenticeship for "new frees" meant working forty hours a week for former owners. Only thirteen hours of this labour was remunerated. With this money, a former slave could more rapidly buy his freedom. However, the system of apprenticeship failed and after four years, on 1 August 1838, Emancipation Day was celebrated and 13,300 slaves tasted real freedom.

At that time St. Lucia was administered, along with other British territories in the West Indies, by a governor-general residing in Barbados.

The need for manual labour to work the sugar estates became apparent at this time. Former slaves were unwilling to return to plantation life and in 1840, sixty-two free Africans came to St. Lucia. They made little impression on the labour shortage and in 1882, the British authorised the entry of the first Indian immigrants.

They came from the Indian sub-continent, particularly the provinces of Uttar Pradesh and Bihar, and were brought in for an initial period of five years. When their service expired, they were offered a choice of ten acres of land or ten pounds sterling. If they signed up for a further five years, they were given their passage back to India. Over a quarter of the Indians who came to St. Lucia opted to return home.

In 1885, the year when Grenada became the government headquarters of the British Windward Islands, attempts were made to diversify the economy

Top: The waters of the Atlantic pound the east coast of St. Lucia. Above: Visitors are greeted by an island nation of welcoming and charming people.

away from its agricultural base. Modern shipping wharves were built at the port of Castries and St. Lucia became a major coaling depot in the Caribbean. Between 1880 and 1930, the port accommodated more than 1,000 steamships, all calling in for refuelling. However, with the introduction of oil, the coaling station became defunct.

The advent of the 20th century was marked by a period of great unrest. In 1906, Britain removed her troops and shut down her naval garrison in St. Lucia and the coal carriers went on strike in 1907. Planters, still looking for a viable alternative to sugar, experimented with sea-island cotton as a new cash crop. But for real success they would have to wait until the 1920s for bananas to be introduced on a large scale.

Left: The Enbas Saut hike through the rainforest reveals a sparkling waterfall that cascades into a crystalline pool below. Above: Hibiscus is commonly seen throughout the Caribbean, with over 200 known species and a grand and varied range of colours.

In the early 1900s, the construction of the Panama Canal, the gold rush in British Guyana and the discovery of oil in the Dutch Antilles caused mass emigration out of St. Lucia as prospectors were lured away with dreams of an easy fortune. Gradually world events began to have a ripple effect even in this quiet corner of the globe and islanders were unable to ignore the inevitable consequences.

In 1913, the first car was imported onto the island and, in 1929, the first airmail service came to St. Lucia by a Pan American seaplane piloted by Colonel Lindbergh. St. Lucia, despite its remote location, went to fight in World War I and thirty-seven nationals, all members of the British West Indian contingent, were killed in action.

St. Lucians also fought in World War II and although the fighting mainly took place on the other side of the Atlantic Ocean, the Caribbean was engaged in military action. The neighbouring island of Martinique, like mainland France, was occupied by the

So many St. Lucians contributed to the British war effort that there was no longer any justification to exclude them from the electoral process, and in 1951 adult franchise was finally granted.

In the post-war period, sugar could no longer sustain the economy and priority was given to banana cultivation. The new monocrop soon became known as "Green Gold". St. Lucian production, the largest of the Windward Islands, found a guaranteed market in Great Britain. Geest, the Dutch multi-national, developed huge plantations in the Roseau Valley and it was on their ships that all the bananas grown in St. Lucia reached England.

In 1960, the Windward Islands government was abolished and St. Lucia received her own constitution and ministerial portfolio.

A further step towards self-determination came in 1967 when the island was granted associated statehood with full internal self-government. Britain retained responsibility for defence and foreign affairs.

Twenty-two years later, on 22 February 1979, St. Lucia became a fully independent nation. The Head of State is the British monarch, represented by a governor-general who is nominated by the government of St. Lucia.

General elections are held in St. Lucia every five years. There are seventeen constituencies and elections are contested mainly by two political parties, the St. Lucia Labour Party and the United Workers Party with the occasional independent running for certain seats.

Left: Brightly-coloured reef fish provides a stark contrast against a dense coral outcrop. Below: Spectacular sunset over Reduit Beach.

Nazi-controlled Vichy government. St. Lucia was protected by the British and by two American military bases constructed in Gros Islet and in Vieux Fort. The island became a beacon for the French citizens in Martinique who heard General de Gaulle's call to arms in 1940 to liberate France.

Under cover of the night, Martiniquans fled to St. Lucia and Dominica using sail-powered *gommier* canoes. These freedom fighters braved the German naval cannons trained on Martinique in order to reach St. Lucia.

The parliamentary system is based on the Westminster model, but a Senate, made up of government and opposition appointees, debates house bills. St. Lucia is also a member of the British Commonwealth.

The island has been an English-speaking nation for nearly 200 years now. Yet, despite the abolition of the French language in the early 1900s, many of the place names still remain predominantly French. The names of towns and communities have all reverted back to their pre-Revolution titles.

St. Lucia also retains her French flavour with the widely-spoken Creole language. This tongue, common to French-speaking islands such as Martinique, Guadeloupe and Haiti, used to be a uniquely oral tradition. It is now a written language and can even be studied at certain universities in the Caribbean.

The population is a cultural blend of African, East Indian, European and Syrian. Despite ethnic differences, most people simply refer to themselves as St. Lucians. As inhabitants of a small autonomous nation, St. Lucians have had to develop a sense of independence and self-reliance. However, they remain to this day some of the most charming and hospitable people in the Caribbean.

There are ten urban centres on the island. Castries, the capital, is where nearly half of the island's 150,000 inhabitants live. The other large population centres are Gros Islet in the north and Vieux Fort to the extreme south. Anse La Raye, Canaries, Soufrière, Choiseul and Laborie are the major villages on the West coast while Micoud and Dennery are the largest communities on the Atlantic. They are all located at

Top left: Always hospitable, St. Lucians will offer a warm greeting to visitors. Left: "Green Gold" – St. Lucia is the largest producer of bananas in the Windward Islands. Above: Cocoa is an important cash crop for the island.

river mouths and their histories are intertwined with the sea and agricultural commerce.

St. Lucia's economy has been described as the most balanced in the Lesser Antilles. The agricultural industry, still heavily dependent on bananas, is being diversified. With Britain's entry into the European Union, St. Lucia's bananas no longer enjoy their protected status. Prices have fallen and the marketplace is open to competition from Latin American and African bananas. Geest has sold its plantations to local farmers.

The coconut industry is being revived and bi-products are used to manufacture edible oils and soaps. Citrus fruits and vegetables are shipped around the Caribbean and to the West Indian communities in North America, Canada and the UK. Locally-grown cut flowers and potted palms are sold on the European market. There is an expanding light manufacturing sector and offshore banking is also being developed.

St. Lucia is one of the largest transhipment points for containerised cargo in the Eastern Caribbean. The old colonial motto *statio haud malefidia carinis* – a

safe haven for ships – still applies to the island.

However, tourism is the largest foreign exchange earner. St. Lucia continues to develop a diversified holiday industry which offers everything from large resorts to small, intimate inns. While the beauty of the island's beaches speaks for itself, tourist activities are not confined to the seaside. The rainforest awaits exploration and there are botanical gardens to visit, horse riding trails to explore, as well as marine parks, nature reserves and national parks to enjoy.

Most of the island is accessible via a network of paved roads.

Locations that remain inaccessible today are all the better for their

isolation. These are wild and rugged places where Mother Nature reigns supreme.

Indeed, much of St. Lucia is mountainous and difficult to reach and almost half of the population has had to build their homes on slopes.

But it is this untamed quality that is St. Lucia's main attraction. Even though the island is much calmer than during its first creative convulsions, (the island's visible volcanic crater at Soufrière is advertised as the world's only "drive-in volcano"), the feeling that Mother Nature is still in control permeates the entire island.

Below: The stone ruins at Pigeon Island National Park include an old kitchen, hospital and military barracks.

a sightseeing

Paradise – a simple word that conjures up many divergent images in the mind of an individual: a euphemism for that perfect time and place – the ultimate dream. To some it is a quiet moment on a secluded beach shaded by coconut palms gently swaying in the breeze and the song of the waves upon the sands. Others envisage such exhilarating experiences such as hiking to the summit of Gros Piton to commune with God and be overwhelmed by the fantastic views; or splashing into an emerald pool rimmed by magnificent vegetation beneath the plunging waters of a mountain waterfall. Perhaps an unrivalled romantic encounter set on a warm night stage with the full moon shimmering on the open sea, witnessed only by the stars; or simply a moment of sincere joy shared with most cherished friends enjoying good food, good drink and good fun in a tropical setting. No matter what your description of that consummate reverie – St. Lucia is definitely the place to find it.

This island offers myriad opportunities and unparalleled places to explore. Fun-filled activities, exciting discoveries, educational enrichment and

spectacular

tranquil memories – they are all to be enjoyed on the mystical "Helen of the West Indies".

There are several ways to see the island. For those who prefer to strike out alone, a rental car or jeep is the answer. Not all the roads are marked, but do not be deterred, as it is difficult to get lost. Take a map and look for assistance along the way – simply ask for the next village along on the map and you will know that you are on the right track. However, be cautious of anybody on the road who may suggest they ride with you and act as your guide for the day. A polite refusal is the safest and easiest way to deal with this situation.

If you are a little sceptical about heading out completely on your own, but want to avoid the larger groups on guided tours, then book a taxi. The certified drivers stationed at the hotels, airports and shopping locations have all completed special courses on tourism and defensive driving and are governed by published official rates. The drivers are also good at suggesting "off the beaten track" locations.

Various tour companies offer packages for half- and full-day trips to almost every part of the island.

The choices are many, so research the areas you want to visit carefully and select your tour guide accordingly.

For general sightseeing, consider the day sails to Soufrière or the "land and sea" trips: both are excellent. The tours generally include the Diamond Mineral Baths, Botanical Gardens and Waterfall; the Sulphur Springs and the Pitons.

To experience the wilds, jeep companies offer trips to the rainforest and waterfalls in open-backed, rough-road jeeps. For those wanting a more educational perspective and a serious look at nature, the tours offered through the Forestry Department and National Trust are best.

Sightseeing experiences on St. Lucia can be enriching and wonderful fun. Please, however, bear in mind that St. Lucian customs may be slightly different to those you are accustomed to at home. Therefore, sit back and enjoy the experience –

remembering that life here moves a little more slowly than you may be accustomed to, but then you *are* on vacation! Relax and enjoy the flow; island life is always *irie*.

Few facilities are equipped to handle wheelchairs and other special requirements, but the local people are very accommodating and most public places do have some areas that can be navigated with assistance. If in doubt, telephone ahead and you will find a unique willingness to help with any special needs.

Left: The sparkling waters of the Diamond Falls on the award-winning Soufrière Estate. Below: The Morne Coubaril Estate gives visitors the chance to witness life on a working plantation.

Pigeon Island National Park and Museum

Turn left just north of Gros Islet village. If you reach Cap Estate, you have gone too far.

Operated by the St. Lucia National Trust.

Telephone: 450-8167

Fax: 450-0060

Hours: Daily from 8:00a.m. to 5:00p.m.

Entrance fee: Minimal

Facilities: Broad, well-maintained paths traverse the main park. There is some wheelchair access. The higher paths are narrower and steeper and should be tackled only by those with average to good levels of fitness. There is a small but well-designed and informative museum that provides a fascinating insight into the history of the park. A small historical guide book is available. There is a casual and relaxed restaurant situated on the beachfront, and a pub in the cellar of one of the old military buildings.

A visit to Pigeon Island National Park will reveal many well-preserved ruins, an informative museum containing numerous military artefacts, as well as a tranquil blend of nature and beauty.

Pigeon Island National Park, known as "the most historical site of the Caribbean" is a relaxing, peaceful blend of history, nature and beauty. The small island sits off the northern coast of St. Lucia, only 2 miles (3 km) north of Rodney Bay. Easy access is provided by a man-made causeway, which was built in 1970 with materials dredged from the nearby marina. Some tours include Pigeon Island, but to truly appreciate its natural splendour and intriguing history, the island is best explored at your own pace with no rush. It makes a perfect half-day excursion, although be sure to pre-arrange your taxi for the return trip.

The park is easily located for those with their own transport and can also be reached using the Rodney Bay Ferry, which operates from the Reduit Beach area in front of the Rex St. Lucian Hotel. Pigeon Island is actually within walking distance from the Rodney Bay and Cap Estate areas, but if you are planning on spending a few hours exploring the park, it is advisable to avoid this additional effort.

The tour begins amidst the stone ruins, which include the old kitchen/hospital and soldiers' barracks. The main path, as it winds upward to the southern peak, leads to Fort Rodney, which was constructed in 1778. The broad path is easily accessible, except for the last 50 yards (45 metres), where some moderate climbing is required.

After exploring the underground powder store at the fort, take a few moments to savour the incredible views from this point. It is well worth taking this climb on a clear day, but it is sensible not to tackle it in the midday sun. To the north lies the southern portion of Martinique. The main reason Admiral Rodney insisted on establishing a naval base here was to keep an ever-watchful eye on the French naval forces at Fort Royal across the water. Looking back towards the causeway, the sandy bays dazzle against the sparkling turquoise waters that meld into deeper regions of intense sapphire. Inland, the view of the dynamic mountain range is staggering.

Admiral de Grasse – headed northward, the British navy set sail from Pigeon Island in close pursuit. The two forces clashed off the small islands between Guadeloupe and Dominica – the Islands of the Saints – with the British defeating the French and saving Jamaica and Admiral Nelson from invasion.

For those willing to endure a further hike, Signal Hill offers more of a challenge. This trek is more arduous as it winds through the steep rocks, but the vista is adequate reward. It is said that Admiral Rodney used to sit here himself with his eyeglass trained on Martinique.

Many battles and skirmishes were fought in the waters surrounding Pigeon Island – and preparations for the most famous naval battle of Caribbean history began here, although the actual engagement was further north. Due to Rodney's astute observations the French were detected amassing their fleet. And, on 8 April 1782, as that fleet – under the leadership of

In addition to its historical significance, Pigeon Island contains some interesting geological formations, because – as is evident in the reversed strata – the island seems to have flipped over completely at some point during its volcanic creation. Other fascinating facets of the island include the Carib Indian caves, a documented, yet still mysterious pirate story and a whaling station. In addition to the main trails, other paths along the

water's edge reveal numerous wonders. The key is to not rush this trip, but relax and enjoy it at your own pace.

There are also delightful well-cultivated gardens where many floral species abound, including a few not widely found across the main island, such as the pencil cedar. Lively bird life rounds out the area's bountiful offerings.

The *Jambe de Bois Restaurant* provides welcome refreshment and a charming setting for a casual beachside lunch. Visitors can enjoy a dip while waiting for their meal. Alternatively, step back into the days of Admiral Rodney by visiting the *Captain Cellar's Pub*, which is housed in the cellar of the original mess hall.

Union Nature Trail

The Union Nature Trail is the ideal spot for visitors who are looking to experience some of the enchanting natural habitat that exist on St. Lucia without enduring an extensive hike or long drive. This tour is perfect for families with smaller children. It also offers a fascinating insight into local herbal remedies and guarantees a glimpse of St. Lucia's wildlife.

At the interpretation centre there is a series of booklets and posters available, including an excellent set of posters detailing the bird life of the island. This is where visitors meet up with their guide.

The mini-zoo is small, but nicely designed. The St. Lucian parrots on display include a pair returned from the Jersey Zoo. These endangered birds are still found in the wild thanks to conservation efforts by the Forestry Department and the Jersey Wildlife Protection Trust, who brought these creatures back from the brink of extinction.

A colony of agouti, the little rodents introduced to the island by the early Arawak settlers, also thrives within the protection of the zoo. In the wild, however, they are at the mercy of boa constrictors and dogs, and only a few remain in isolated areas. The indigenous iguana is also seen here, along with a fine specimen of the island's own species of boa constrictor.

A short and easy walk through latanier palms, a larger variety of

the plants from which the local brooms are fashioned brings you to the medicinal garden. Developed by the Forestry Division, it provides a most interesting look at the cultural diversities of St. Lucia merging into one people through the traditional uses of plants as medicine. The story begins with the Amerindians, who used the seeds of the *woucou* plant which produced an oily red substance to make ceremonial body paint.

The medicinal garden provides a fascinating insight into the tradition of herbal remedies. Since the ancient days of the Amerindian settlers, plants have yielded natural medicines and hope of life. Visitors can discover some unique uses for the island's spices and herbs.

The nature trail winds along the hillside and is not difficult to negotiate, although it does involve some climbing. The well-shaded path leads through a shrub forest containing some interesting trees – all marked for easy identification. Bird watching is best in the early morning or late afternoon.

Rodney Bay

The area around Rodney Bay is the location of the fabulous Reduit Beach and the home of many of St. Lucia's hotels and restaurants. Rodney Bay has, in recent years, been a site of continual development. The JQ Shopping Mall opened here in late 1998 and is the home of many interesting shops, as well as a well-stocked supermarket. The Rodney Bay Marina is the finest full service facility in the eastern Caribbean.

Reduit Beach is the island's most popular beach and most watersports are available here. The magnificent *Royal St. Lucian Hotel* fronts the beach and is a

great place to visit for an excellent lunch or dinner. There are many other restaurants in the area, including *Memories of Hong Kong, Razmatazz, Capone's* and *Spinnakers* which is located directly on the beach. (*See Eat Your Heart Out, page 138*).

There are also a number of exciting bars to visit including the *Lime,*

Shamrocks and *Indies.* (*See Where to Get Uncorked, page 122*). A mix of locals and tourists frequent these lively places which are humming on Friday and Saturday nights.

In nearby Gros Islet, the weekly jump-up attracts revellers from all over the island. There is a great party atmosphere and you can eat fish or chicken grilled on roadside braziers. The music is loud, the beer is cold and the streets are packed however for the visitor who wants to party late into the night, this is the place to be.

Marquis Estate

The estate is located on the north-eastern coastline just past the village of Boguis.

Transportation is provided for visitors on tour packages.

Telephone: For the plantation tour 452-8232

For the horse riding 450-0197

Fax: For the plantation tour 452-8683

E-mail: For the horse riding countrysaddles@candw.lc

Hours: By organized tour only.

Entrance fee: Included in the tour rates.

Facilities: Meals and drinks are provided according to the tour package. Wheelchair facilities are not available but some accommodations can be made. Visitors who have completed riding courses for the disabled are welcome if no special equipment is required.

The Marquis Plantation is one of the oldest sugar estates on the island. The sugar mill and associated buildings date back to the 1770s and are still reasonably intact. The history of the area is fascinating and begins in 1723 with the Marquis de Champigny who landed in the bay with 1400 men. They cut a straight path across the interior mountains to join troops at Choc Bay. The British immediately discovered they were surrounded and outnumbered, and no battle was fought. This manoeuvre resulted in the Treaty of Choc.

During the years when the estate was a working sugar plantation, it was also home to the French governor. This was primarily because Dauphin, the bay just to the north, housed the French capital. The ridge adjoining the two bays was fortified to protect both the capital and the governor. Small, spiked cannons are on display in front of the old estate house, and were most likely left behind after de Champigny's march or by the governor's residency.

The plantation tour takes in the old sugar buildings where some of the original equipment is on display, including giant wooden vats used in sugar production and a press used in the making of lime juice.

A short boat ride down the Marquis River takes in the enchanting river habitat through the mangrove to the waters of the Atlantic Ocean and a small bay edged by steep cliffs. Back at

the plantation house – recently owned by Lord Walston of Great Britain, but currently owned by a St. Lucian family, the Atkinsons – a tasty traditional lunch is served.

The Great Horse Adventure, operated by Country Saddles at the Marquis Estate, is a fantastic sightseeing opportunity down through the plantation, lush banana fields and verdant forest area to the beach.

The Marquis Estate is located in a tranquil, country setting and offers a sample of some unique island history and wildlife. It is advisable to telephone in advance to reserve space on the tours, which are only available on selected days.

Photographs: The Marquis Plantation offers visitors the chance to enjoy a glimpse of a bygone era, as well as ride through banana fields to an isolated east coast beach.

Castries

Castries, the bustling capital, is the only city on St. Lucia. The main settlement was originally on the opposite side of the harbour at Vigie. It was then named *Le Carenage*, which literally translates into "a place where boats were pulled ashore for careening and care". At that time the area was largely swamp area – much land having been reclaimed since – which unfortunately promoted ill health. The village was later moved to its present location and its name changed in 1785 to Castries – after the Marechal de Castries, a French colonial minister who was the governor of the island in 1784.

In 1948, eight per cent of Castries was destroyed by a raging fire that reputedly began in a small tailor's shop. The city of today, therefore, reflects very little of the colonial atmosphere and buildings that existed prior to the disaster, although a fine example of the Victorian-style architecture is the **Rain Restaurant** on Brazil Street, decorated with delicate filigree latticework.

The **market** was constructed between 1891–94 and has been recently renovated. New sections of the market give it a cheery West Indian flavour and the bustling activity is a constant swirl of colour, heady aromas and lively banter amongst the vendors. Visitors will enjoy this fascinating look at the wealth of local produce

available, including exotic fruits and vegetables and sweet-smelling herbs and spices. Upstairs, island crafts are on sale, including locally-made baskets and pottery.

In the centre of the city is **Derek Walcott Square**. It was renamed in honour of the renowned St. Lucian author after he won the 1992 Nobel Prize for Literature. There is a war memorial in the centre of the square and an imposing 400-year-old saman tree, which provides welcome respite from the heat of the sun. One of the most impressive buildings in Castries is the **Cathedral of the Immaculate**

Above: Castries and the cruise ship terminal of Point Seraphine. Left: Vendor selling fresh hot peppers. Centre: The murals in the Cathedral of the Immaculate Conception are by Dunstan St. Omer. Right: The interior of the cathedral.

Conception, located on the east side of Derek Walcott Square. It was built in 1894, due to the perseverance of Father Tapon, whose great nephew later became the first bishop of the cathedral.

It has an iron-work and wooden interior and brightly painted roof. The murals around the interior colourfully portray the cathedral in the history of St. Lucia. The paintings were created by Dunstan St. Omer, one the country's foremost artists who has created some unique works of art. He is renowned for his bold style and contemporary techniques.

The main **library** is on the opposite side of the square and is housed in an impressive Victorian building. Further along Laborie Street is the modern **Court** and **Parliament** buildings and the tiny **Constitution Park**. The main business and shopping area is centred around **William Peter Boulevard**, where the main banks,

airline offices, tour operators and general stores are located.

The **Pointe Seraphine** cruise ship terminal is located along the John Compton Highway. The road leads past the government offices and the unusually-shaped headquarters of the Alliance Française. A selection of boutiques stock designer clothing, jewellery, electronics, perfumes and a vast array of souvenir items. Pointe Seraphine, the larger of the two duty-free complexes, is just north of harbour and **La Place Carenage** is located wharf side in Castries.

Pointe Seraphine (open 9:00a.m. to 5:00p.m. from Monday to Friday and from 9:00a.m. to 2:00p.m. on Saturday) would be the shopping centre of choice if time allows.

Carry your passport and airline ticket or cruise ship boarding pass as these documents are necessary in order to receive your duty free allowance.

The Spanish style architecture with its open courtyards provides a pleasant atmosphere for a morning of shopping. The shops include names such as Beneton, Little Switzerland and Colombian Emeralds. Shops with a more local flair include Bagshaws, with their colourful array of silkscreen items, and Natur Pur Designer Clothing who sell a range of comfortable clothing.

Morne Fortune, meaning the "hill of good luck", sits behind Castries and offers splendid views across the city to the harbour. It was used throughout colonial history as a fortification for Castries Harbour and was named Fort Charlotte by the British. A turning just as the road reaches the hill leads past the old

yellow brick British barracks to the small Provost Redoubt, rimmed by the more ancient French stone ruins (thought to be remnants of the prison and stable). Driving through the grounds of Sir Arthur Lewis Community College, you will see a cannon marking the location of the Inniskilling Monument, which can be reached by taking a short stroll along the palm-lined pathway. This spot is where the bloodiest battle ever fought in St. Lucia took place on 24 May 1796, when the 27th Foot Royal Inniskilling Fusiliers – led by Captain Moore – repelled the French revolutionary forces and secured the fort.

Captain Moore subsequently took over the possibly even more difficult challenge – that of returning slaves into bondage. Imagine the ferocity of men freed by the Revolution now ordered to return to their lives of slavery. The resistant forces, known as Brigands, waged a guerrilla-type warfare against the British. The eventual solution, after many months and much bloodshed, was to band the men together and dub them the "First West Indies Regiment".

Winding around the hill behind the college, the road passes an old powder store, cleverly designed to resemble a chapel. The walls of this building are extremely thick and were constructed with an air vent between two sections to keep the ammunition cool and dry. Continuing the circle around the Morne, the road leads to the Four Apostle's Battery, a more modern fortification constructed by the British during the late 1800s in conjunction with the La Toc Battery, a restored fort of the same period.

La Toc Battery is located between Bagshaws Studio and Sandals St. Lucia Resort. (Tel: 452-7921). This fortification was constructed by the British in 1865 as part of a series of reinforcements for Castries Harbour, which was a major coaling station for the British fleet at the time. It consisted of two gun batteries, a look-out station, a main artillery level, underground powder store rooms and a long tunnel.

The technology of this era is fascinating, ranging from the unique lifts to the extensive and still-functioning drainage systems and the artillery. The original cannons, one of which remains on the site, were the first rifled barrels ever manufactured. These massive 10-inch (25-cm) rifled-muzzle loaders were important for the British as their introduction coincided with the creation of the French iron-clad ships.

The fort has been authentically restored to recreate the atmosphere of the period, complete with twinkling lanterns in the underground rooms and the tunnel which led to the front of the fort in case of enemy landing. As the fort's main function was to protect the southern entrance to the harbour, the view from here is panoramic and remarkable.

As World War I approached, the British began to withdraw their forces in preparation for the fighting in Europe. The fort was abandoned in 1905, without a shot ever having been fired. This site is highly recommended for those with even a vague interest in military history.

There is a collection of antique bottles on display, many of which were found in the waters that surround the island during the underwater expeditions of Alice Bagshaw. Alice has been the driving force behind the restoration of the fort and is the proprietor of the nearby Bagshaw's Silkscreening Studio.

Marigot Bay

Located approximately 10 miles (16 km) south of Castries (turn right just before the Roseau Valley).

Entrance fee: A small fee for the ferry, which provides the only access to the other side of the bay.

Facilities: Although there is no official wheelchair access, it is possible to board the ferry with some lifting over small steps. *Doolittles Restaurant* provides casual dining at the Marigot Beach Club on the far side of the bay. The *Moorings Restaurant*, located on the near side of the bay, is slightly more formal than *Doolittles*.

Marigot Bay epitomizes the phrase "tropical paradise". The setting is exquisite: a hilltop view above the bay overlooks the steeply-sloping hillside and the serene waters beyond, gilded by swaying palms and fringed by mangrove. The area is dotted with many colourful yachts, as this is the home of Moorings Yachting Centre. The beauty of Marigot Bay was captured in many tropical scenes in the film *Dr. Doolittle*.

The bay is so secluded it has been dubbed "Hurricane Hole", meaning that it is a safe anchorage during blustery weather. There is also a legend that gives Marigot Bay a place in history. During the Battle of Cul de Sac in 1778, when Admiral Barrington was sent to capture St. Lucia from the French, it is reputed that the British Navy being pursued by the French – dipped into Marigot Bay. They camouflaged their ships by lashing palm fronds to their vessels and the French sailed past – seeing only a coconut grove along the far side of the bay. The British were then able to return north, land at Cul de Sac, and secure the island for the Union Jack.

Roseau – a drive-by photo stop

The Roseau Valley, just south of Cul de Sac, is best viewed from the look-out post to the south. From here the expansive vista takes in the old rum factory, the verdant banana fields to the north, the wetlands below and the pretty beach, sometimes complete with brightly-coloured fishing boats.

Above: Bird's-eye view of Marigot Bay – a safe haven for yachts during bad weather. Below: Brightly-painted boats reflect in the serene waters at Marigot Bay.

La Sikwi (Ingervoll) Estate

Just before the bridge entering Anse La Raye from the north, turn left towards the Ingervoll Estate. Bear right at the junction, which leads to a footbridge over the river.

Telephone: 452-6323

Hours: 8:00a.m. to 4:00p.m. Monday to Saturday.

Entrance fee: Minimal

Facilities: Garden bar. Wheelchair access to gardens and bar areas. Lunches are provided for groups of a minimum of ten people. They must be reserved in advance.

Above: La Sikwi Estate was constructed in 1876 and is surrounded by lush tropical gardens. Right: Some of the original milling machinery on display at the estate.

This is one of the few sugar mills on the island built by the British. Constructed in 1876, it is slightly more modern than the original French buildings. It remains in excellent condition with much of the original milling machinery in place, including the 40-foot (12-metre) waterwheel.

The sugar mill produced molasses as its final product, not refined sugar. Molasses were in high demand, especially in the manufacture of rum. During the early 1900s the factory was transformed into lime oil production. Today, the Ingervoll Estate grows bananas, cocoa and some coffee.

The guided tour includes a detailed explanation of both sugar cane and lime oil processing. The factory has been adorned with original tools and pieces of machinery, along with old photographs and postcards. A stroll through the idyllic gardens ends the tour with a look at many common and a few exotic island botanical species. The majestic setting is in the shadow of an imposing mountain. There is also a small theatre for special events.

This location is included on the Jungle Tours (telephone 450-0434) and Jeep Safari Tours excursions. Both organisations take their visitors into the wild in open-back jeeps. Walk-in visitors are also welcome. The road is easily navigable by rental car or taxi. It is an excellent excursion, especially when combined with one of the nearby waterfalls and a tour of the neighbouring village of Anse La Raye.

Anse La Raye to Soufrière

A pretty coastal village along the west coast road between Castries and Soufrière, south of Roseau and north of Canaries.

This small fishing village has, as a result of great community effort, developed several interesting attractions. Along the water's edge visitors will find a display of local canoe-making. This ancient art stems from the original Amerindian techniques, which involved charring the inside wood to make it easier to chip out and then filling the boat with rocks and water for weeks to help widen the shape.

The village wall is a museum in itself. A colourful mural details local life mastered in bright strokes by the artist Dunstan St. Omer. He is responsible for the many vibrant portraits in local churches including those in the Cathedral of the Immaculate Conception in Castries.

Look out for the local bakeries selling freshly-baked Creole loaves for the perfect mid-morning snack. Passing through town and crossing the bridge, you may find some local ladies doing their weekly wash in the river. As the road starts to climb just south of the village, there is a excellent photo opportunity of the view back into the bay, which takes in rows of colourful boats and fishing nets drying in the sun.

The Saturday night fish-fry is becoming an increasingly popular event on St. Lucia. It is similar to the fish-fry held every Friday at Oistins on Barbados. Visitors are encouraged to join the local fishing community when they set up cooking facilities on street corners around the town.

The road between Anse La Raye and the village of Canaries hugs the mountain range that rises into vast expanses of rainforest on one side and drops down to the sparkling waters of the Caribbean Sea on the other. The twin peaks of the majestic Pitons are visible from various points along the route to Soufrière, but the last part of the journey – as the road leads down the winding hillside towards this picturesque fishing town – is the most breathtaking.

Beyond the town, the Pitons rise out of the sea like immense tropical pyramids. The water's edge is fringed with graceful palms and black sands. These are indicative of the volcanic activity in the area.

Above: The picturesque fishing village of Anse La Raye.

Soufrière

The town of Soufrière nestles in a valley beneath Petit Piton. It was a thriving port in the 18th century and is one of the oldest settlements on St. Lucia. There are many petroglyphs to be found in the area which was first inhabited by the Amerindians. Soufrière was the first town to be established in St. Lucia and has remained an important farming centre ever since. It was badly hit by a hurricane in 1780 that devastated most of the town and many of the nearby sugar and coffee plantations. It then became embroiled in the French Revolution of 1789. The

Above: The pretty town of Soufrière sits in the shadow of the majestic Pitons. Right: Colourful wooden houses are shaded by palms on the water's edge in Soufrière.

town was renamed *La Convention* by the Revolutionary Council in Paris and a guillotine was erected in the town square.

The town today is quite dilapidated, although its strong French heritage can still be seen in many of the buildings and places nearby. There are charming old wooden houses decorated with gingerbread fretwork, as well as craft centres, shops and restaurants. There is a market on Saturday morning on the waterfront, although the area is a hive of activity on most afternoons when the local fishermen sell their daily catch.

Soufrière is also renowned as the home of Marie-Joseph-Rose de Tascher de la Pagerie – better known as Empress Josephine, wife of Napoleon Bonaparte. She spent much of her childhood at her father's estate, *Malmaison*, on the outskirts of the town.

To the north of Soufrière, the stunning beach of Anse Chastanet sits at the end of a steep and rough road. The reefs in this area are some of the most magnificent in the Caribbean because of the myriad tropical fish, fantastic corals and colourful sponges. *(See Underwater Extravaganza, page 72).*

The Sulphur Springs

The road south and inland along the main west coast road leads to the Sulphur Springs. This area is operated by the Soufrière Foundation.

Telephone: 459-7686

Fax: 459-7999

Hours: 9:00a.m. to 5:00p.m. Monday to Sunday.

Entrance fee: Minimal.

Facilities: There is a small snack shop. Visitors must be accompanied by a guide. The tour involves a walk requiring a moderate level of fitness.

The Sulphur Springs are a wonder of natural geology. The site is known as the "world's only drive-in volcano". Visitors used to be allowed to walk among the steaming, boiling pools. However, after an accident involving one of the guides, viewing stations have since been installed.

More technically the area is classified as a *caldera*, or rather a portion of the volcanic rim that

Right: The Sulphur Springs are made up of twenty-four bubbling cauldrons where a portion of the volcanic rim collapsed and opened fissures in the crust.

has collapsed in on itself, opening fissures in the crust. This allows for the constant escape of steam through the twenty-four bubbling cauldrons, preventing the build-up of pressure which would cause an eruption. Due to this remarkable natural pressure valve, the *Qualibu Caldera* is classified as dormant. Research by volcanologist Frank Perret in 1940 found the formation to be "the most interesting: perhaps the most potentially active" when compared to other calderas around the globe.

As you enter the area, one of the first things you notice is the acrid sulphur fumes. Whilst this is somewhat unpleasant to the senses, sulphur is exceptionally beneficial to one's health and has long been recognized as being helpful in the treatment of sinusitis, arthritis and skin problems. The knowledgeable guides escort visitors along the walkway to the various look-outs and explain the geological history of the area and how the landscape was created. They also explain the other minerals present in the waters and rocks, as well as past attempts at harnessing the awesome power of the Sulphur Springs into geothermal energy.

As you peer into the dark grey pits of bubbling water and steaming vapour, you will be able to identify with the Carib Indians who gave the place its name, *Qualibu* – "the place of death". It is essential to stay within the boundary fences, as the ground around the pools is very dangerous.

Soufrière Estate

A five-minute drive south from the town of Soufrière.

Telephone: 459-7565 or 452-4759

Fax: 453-2068

Hours: 10:00a.m. to 5:00p.m. for the Diamond Mineral Baths, Botanical Gardens and Waterfall. Visitors may tour the Soufrière Estate by prior appointment only.

Entrance fee: There is a nominal charge for the garden and an additional fee for bathing.

Facilities: The paths are generally wheelchair accessible for most areas of the gardens.

The Soufrière Estate is one of the oldest plantations on the island. The land, an area of 2,000 acres (810 hectares), was granted to the Devaux family by King Louis XIV in 1713. The family arrived in 1742 to establish their home, and the same family still owns the plantation today. The mill was built in 1765 for sugar production and later was used to crush limes. The old water-wheel has been restored to working order and is a remarkable feat of engineering. The factory itself has been transformed into a picturesque restaurant with the restorations being recognized by the 1996 American Express Caribbean Preservation Award.

The driveway to the restaurant is lined with traditional crops such as cocoa, as well as dense lush tropical flora. The buffet luncheons are excellent offering a choice of fresh fish or chicken accompanied by a variety of salads and tasty local vegetables, many grown on the estate. Dessert is generally a sampling of local fruits. Lunches are available by prior appointment only, with at least twelve hours' notice required. This superb meal is definitely worth the effort of advance reservations.

The adjacent Diamond Mineral Baths, Botanical Gardens and Waterfall are owned and lovingly run by the same management – the dynamic Joan Devaux. Her hard-working and continued efforts have turned both properties into one of the best tourist sites on the island; a special combination of history and natural delights.

A tour of the garden begins with a path meandering along the stream bed. The waters, blackened with minerals from the Sulphur Springs, provide evidence of the volcanic activity stirring deep below the earth's crust. The plants are labelled with common names, and plaques throughout

the gardens detail the history of the falls and baths. A great variety of botanical orders are represented here, including a mixture of propagated spices such as vanilla beans and nutmeg alongside aesthetic beauties such as lilies, bird of paradise and anthuriums. Look for the torch lily, an odd variety appearing to be fashioned from wax.

A side path slips through the tranquil water garden exhibiting lily pads and other aquatic plants.

The sound of the water as it trickles over the rocks generates some relaxing background effects whilst viewing this charming section of the gardens.

Further along, the path reaches the site of the baths. The original stone baths were commissioned by King Louis XIV in 1784 to provide his troops with easy access to the numerous health benefits of the mineral waters. They stand beside the more modern plunge pools and bathing is possible for an additional fee.

A table outside the small gift and snack shop displays many local spices and produce. A lady dressed in national costume is on hand to provide identification and explanations concerning their use.

For the grand finale, a walk through dense foliage leads to the Diamond Falls. This medium-sized waterfall cascades over rocks coloured many different hues by the minerals present in the waters. The falls tumble into

a boulder-lined pool and then continue along the moss-covered stones of the stream.

The Soufrière Estate, with its Diamond Mineral Baths, Botanical Gardens and Waterfall, is included on many tours around St. Lucia, including the fun-filled day trips by catamaran to Soufrière. These day sails are great sightseeing trips that offer a little of everything. However for those wishing to enjoy a fabulous lunch, a dip in the mineral baths and the opportunity to explore the splendid gardens at leisure, then a do-it-yourself trip by rental car or taxi is suggested.

Far left: Colourful ixora abound throughout the Soufrière Estate. Top left: The luxuriant gardens of the estate. Left: The original mineral baths were commissioned by King Louise XIV. Above: Shady trees line the route to the Diamond Falls.

Morne Coubaril Estate

Located about two miles south of Soufrière on the road to the fishing village of Choiseul.

Telephone: 459-7340

Fax: 459-5759

Hours: 9:00a.m. to 5:00p.m. Monday to Saturday.

Entrance fee: Reasonable

Facilities: The Pitt Restaurant is by reservation only. Horseback riding and rainforest hikes are available at additional fees.

Morne Coubaril is situated high in the mountains in the shadow of the Pitons. This estate gives visitors the opportunity to see at first hand some of the island's traditional agricultural activities. It is a working plantation, with the crops grown and processed in the grounds. The cocoa is polished in large copper kettles by the cocoa dance – a traditional practice where a person stands in the pot of beans and polishes them with quick movements of the feet. The farina is dried in similar kettles, and the copra (dried coconut) is baked in small ovens called copra houses. The authentically restored plantation village adds another time and dimension to the atmosphere and visitors are invited to participate in a number of activities which date back a century or more.

A wonderful rainforest hike is also available from Morne Coubaril, but this must be booked in advance. The two-hour trek begins at the Botanical Gardens in Soufrière and winds through the cocoa fields along the Coubaril Stream. The highlight of the walk is the Coubaril Falls where a mixture from the warm sulphur springs and fresh water cascade into the pool below. Visitors are able to bathe in the luxuriant waters and ease their tired muscles.

Back at the estate visitors who have made advance bookings can enjoy a traditional lunch served to the sounds of a lively steel band. The delicious meal includes zesty Creole dishes served with fresh local vegetables including plantain, breadfruit and dasheene, as well as a variety of salads.

Guests are also able to visit the estate's own private stable. From here visitors can enjoy one- or two-hour rides to sites in and around Soufrière. It is also possible to arrange a week-long trail, staying at island guest houses along the route.

Left and below: Coffee is one of the many crops processed at Morne Coubaril. Others include cocoa, copra, manioc and sugar cane. Above: The estate provides an authentic look at plantation life dating back a hundred years.

The Pitons

The twin peaks of the Pitons, as they surge up from the sea bed, have been used to symbolize the uniqueness of St. Lucia for years. These are two volcanic extrusions or plugs – mountains formed by underground volcanic pressure. Petit Piton soars to 2,460 feet (750 metres) and is the closest to Soufrière. It has a small protrusion on its inland face, giving rise to the Amerindian belief that it is the goddess of birth.

Gros Piton reaches a height of 2,619 feet (800 metres) and is also wider in girth than Petit Piton. It was also considered to be a great Amerindian god. A theory is held by many historians of the region – including St. Lucian Robert Devaux – that a three-sided pyramid shape figuring prominently in Amerindian artifacts may be a portrayal of the Pitons, denoting their importance to the early Indians.

It is possible to climb Gros Piton. Hikes, which begin in the village of Fond Gens Libre, are organized by the Department of Forestry. It is a

Above: The magnificent Petit Piton towers over the west coast of St.Lucia.
Right: Traditional crafts are produced at the Choiseul Arts and Crafts Centre.

very strenuous climb and should not be tackled by anybody who is unfit. The magnificent view from the summit is, however, quite spectacular and worth the effort.

Choiseul

A charming fishing village on the southern west coast with a pretty church located virtually on the beach. It is reached along the new road from Soufrière, through the mountains and rainforest and past the Pitons.

This area was the final stand for the last native Caribs of the island. In 1664, the Carib Indians sold St. Lucia to the British living in Barbados and immediately joined forces with them to oust the French, who were occupying the island at the time. The Indians kept their side of the bargain and later left the island in favour of Dominica and St. Vincent. A few,

however, remained, but this time in peaceful harmony with the European settlers. They congregated at the northern peninsula of Choiseul Bay known as La Pointe Caraîbe. *Ajoupas*, the traditional thatched huts of the Indians are still evident today.

As a result of the Carib culture continuing to mingle with that of the new settlers, many traditional crafts remain alive, surviving to be part of today's heritage. The pottery and basket-weaving techniques of the Choiseul area are almost identical to those of the Amerindians. To help protect these crafts for future generations, the Choiseul Arts and Crafts Centre was created. It is open from Monday to Friday from 8am to 4pm and on Saturday from 10am to 4pm.

A further indication of the island's Indian ancestry can be found to the north of the village at Ravine

Chûte d'Eau, where a stream shoots from the rocky heights into the sea. Here, a small petroglyph, (rock carving), of Amerindian origin is visible fairly close to the roadside. It seems to represent a human figure, but is much more primitive than those found at Dauphin and Jalousie – both believed to have been major ceremonial sites.

Laborie

This picturesque fishing village south of Choiseul is particularly known for its lovely seascapes and its black volcanic sands. As it is still an active fishing village, you may be able to purchase fresh fish straight off the boat if you arrive in the late afternoon.

Left: The traditional art of woodcarving is practiced in Choiseul. Below: The pretty village of Laborie is known for its black sands and serene waters.

Balembouche Estate

Located south of Choiseul.

Telephone: 455-1342

Hours: By appointment only and on selected tours.

Facilities: No wheelchair facilities, but the gardens near the house are easily accessed.

Balembouche is one of the finest examples of a traditional plantation house on the island. It is lived in by the owner, Uta Lawaetz and her daughters, and is filled with beautiful wooden furniture and many antiques.

The house sits within majestic grounds and lawns where giant trees spread their shady limbs over old sugar kettles. The original rum-still stands among the grassy reeds, and the exotic flowers are nurtured by Uta herself.

Visitors can stay in one of two exquisitely-designed cottages situated on the estate, or – for those who prefer a more traditional setting – elegant rooms are available in the main house. (See Where to Hang Your Hat, page 128).

A walk along a water path shows sections of the original canal system that fed the sugar mill.

A trip to Balembouche is totally relaxing and visitors can enjoy an enchanting afternoon reminiscent of a bygone era while they enjoy tea and cakes in the immaculate garden, or one of Uta's fabulous home-prepared lunches. The meals are prepared from organically-grown fruits and vegetables from the estate; guests can also dine by candlelight in the dining room or on the veranda overlooking the extensive gardens. The gentle spirit of the owner transforms the property into "home" for all who wander in that direction.

Top left: The plantation house at Balembouche Estate is filled with many antiques. Left and above: The old rum still and parts of the sugar mill can be found within the grounds of the estate.

Maria Island

Located off the east coast of the southern tip of St. Lucia.

Telephone: 453-7656

Fax: 453-2791

Hours: By appointment only. All trips to the island must be accompanied by an official guide.

Entrance fee: Reasonable, including the guide and boat trip.

Facilities: A small interpretation centre gives a brief overview of the islands and their nature. There are restaurants in this area.

The Maria Islands are two small islets off the Atlantic coast close to Vieux Fort in the south of St. Lucia. They are small in size, but gigantic in natural wildlife. Two of the world's rarest creatures have taken a final refuge here. This secret seclusion has not been sought from the unyielding forces of nature, as the Maria Islands are extremely exposed, but from the destructive and encroaching forces of man and civilization.

The Maria Islands Ground Lizard (*zandoli te*) is a lizard which grows to about 14 inches (35 cm) in length. The male's most stunning feature is its brilliant blue tail, although the males found on the smaller island, Maria Minor, are less brilliant in size and colour. The small, harmless *couresse* snake, only found on the larger of the two islands, Maria Major, is hardly ever seen by man as it is very timid and nocturnal. This little snake was once found all over St. Lucia, but suffered the same fate as its close cousin, the black *cribo*, with the introduction of the mongoose. The *cribo* was not fortunate enough to find its way to one of the smaller islets, which is a pity as it was known to consume the poisonous *fer de lance* snake.

In addition to these rare endemic species, the island plays host to several other lizards and numerous birds.

Three types of gecko have been spotted on the island. The rock and pygmy geckos are quite common, but

sightings of the tree gecko have become rare in recent years.

Many coastal birds find sanctuary on the Maria Islands when they are nesting. The sooty and bridle terns lay their eggs seemingly without care along the barren rocks atop the hill, even along the pathway. This is one reason why the park is closed during the nesting season. The brown noddy selects crevices in the cliff edge for more protection against predators and the elements. The red-billed tropic bird spends much time soaring over the open sea, but does come to this spot during the breeding period.

With so much wildlife seeking seclusion and protection from man's interference, please respect what nature has struggled so hard to save.

Top: The male Maria Island Ground Lizard (zandoli te) has a brilliant blue tail. Left: The island is host to many types of lizard.

Errand Plantation

The plantation is just north of Dennery.

Telephone: 452-9842

Fax: 452-9843

Hours: 9:00a.m. to 4:00p.m.

Entrance fee: Reasonable

Facilities: No special facilities for the handicapped, but the grounds can be accessed with assistance. Lunch is only provided for guests on an organized tour.

The official tour to Errand Plantation begins in an all-terrain open-backed jeep. The drive takes about fifty minutes from Castries. Upon arrival at the estate the introductory tour includes a thorough look at cocoa production and nutmeg processing. A walk through the vegetable garden shows the more traditional local produce, and many items that will later appear on the lunch table. A separate kitchen herb garden shows the many commonly-used local seasonings and spices.

The tour is designed with a choice of several walks and experiences

and visitors can decide which one appeals most after viewing the immediate grounds. A short walk leads to a waterfall, while a two-hour trek involves a deeply forested trail. A short excursion in the four-wheel-drive vehicle allows visitors the chance to take a dip in the larger waterfall.

After a splendid lunch prepared in the renovated plantation, the "relaxing trail" is a gentle walk through shady grounds.

Praslin

A small village on the east coast road south of Dennery.

This little village has long been the home of canoe construction – a tradition begun by the Amerindians, even before they embarked on their long sea voyage from South America to the islands. The massive gommier trees are felled in the rainforest,

where some preliminary charring and chipping takes place. When it has been partially dug out the canoe/tree is dragged to the water's edge where weeks more preparation will make it into a seaworthy vessel.

After the core has been properly hollowed, the space is filled with stones and water and then heated. This is left for about six weeks, causing the canoe to expand into the correct shape.

The sides are then built up with planks of white cedar, which has the required natural curve. This tree also provides the inside stays for the canoe. A bright coat of paint finishes the masterpiece, except for the final touch – the personalized name given to it by the new owner.

The canoe building is easily seen from the road, and visitors are welcome to stop and watch the work in progress.

Top: Cocoa beans are dried on racks in the sun. Above: The tradition of canoe building dates back to the Amerindians.

Fregate Island

The island is located on the east coast road between Dennery and Praslin and is operated by the St. Lucia National Trust.

Telephone: 453-7656

Fax: 453-2791

Hours: By appointment only. All visitors must be accompanied by an official guide.

Entrance fee: Reasonable, including the cost of the guide.

Facilities: This is a nature site with no facilities.

Fregate Island Nature Reserve affords a great opportunity to sample some of the natural habitats and wildlife of St. Lucia. The two-hour hike passes through shrub forest, coastal region and mangrove.

The path leading to the small islets of Fregate Major and Minor is lined with stunning cacti of considerable size. The thin syej grows to between 15 and 20 feet (4 and 6 metres) and is found along the point overlooking the small rocky islands. Among the vegetation are primitive Amerindian look-out posts, basically consisting of large boulders placed in a protective, semi-circular formation. Shards of ancient pottery can be found strewn across the ground in these areas.

From the main look-out point visitors can view the islets, as well as the rugged cliffs continually being pounded by the relentless surf.

During the spring months of March to early June, a multitude of frigate birds can usually seen hovering over and fishing among the black rocky slopes. These magnificent black birds have a wingspan of up to 6 feet (2 metres), enabling them to ride the wind currents and stay out to sea for many months at a time. Their wings are so large that it is difficult for them to take off unless they jump off the cliff's edge like a natural hang-glider.

wanders through shrub forest with a flowing stream during the rainy season. Here you may glimpse such rarities as the black finch or St. Lucian oriole among the other, more common forest birds. The ramier, or red-necked pigeon, may even pass overhead.

The Fregate Island Nature Reserve is an opportunity for a pleasant trek, taking in a good variety of local flora and fauna, as well as some dramatic coastal views.

Left: Magnificent frigate bird circles above the sanctuary of Fregate Island. Centre: A view from the east coast across to Fregate Island Nature Reserve. Below: Fregate Island is home to spectacular cacti.

The females and young males have white throat patches. The adult males are all black except in the mating season when the throat plumage turns to a deep scarlet in order to attract the females. The birds have selected the extreme isolation of Fregate Major as their nesting site.

The hike continues along the coastline to a small but attractive mangrove area. Here the guide will point out the various types of the remarkable mangrove tree. Be alert, as this is a favourite spot for the boa constrictor to take its repose, generally slung haphazardly in tree branches. These creatures are not aggresive or poisonous, but will give a nasty bite if harassed. Therefore, feel free to look – but do not touch!

Completing the circle back to the parking area, the trail

Mamiku Gardens

Located at Mon Repos, just past the village of Praslin and only a few minutes off the main road. When travelling south from Castries, watch for signs indicating the right turn.

Telephone: 455-3729

Fax: 452-9023

Hours: 9:00a.m. to 5:00p.m. Monday to Sunday.

Entrance fee: Reasonable

Facilities: A brochure, available at the entrance, includes a general map of the gardens and a numerical list of botanical species. The restaurant and gift shop are centrally located. Lower-level paths are accessible for wheelchairs.

The site of the gardens and nature trail was one of turmoil during the period following the French Revolution. It became a stronghold for the British military against the "Brigands", or rebel slaves. However interesting, the bloody history is hard to picture in the sedate setting of today. The garden boasts over 200 species of flora and has a particularly lovely section displaying numerous orchids.

The main path through the centre section of the gardens is well-suited for anyone of moderate fitness. It slopes gently from one botanical wonder to the next. A small detour leads to the Mystic Garden, which harbours a delicate and colourful collection of orchids. The tiny "Secret Garden" is located higher up and is a wonderful spot for reflection and relaxation.

The trail leading to the heights above has been laid through the nearby natural forest and includes the bois d'Inde tree, a member of the allspice family whose leaves are brewed up by locals as a tea for colds. Benches cleverly fashioned out of logs and branches line the path, and a

bubbling little stream flows through the grounds. A short walk affords a spectacular view of Praslin Bay and is well worth the fifteen-minute hike. The nearby site of the old plantation house is the location of an archaeological dig.

At the base of the hill, the restaurant and shop housed in a plantation-style building offer welcome refreshment.

Top left: The tranquil setting of Mamiku Gardens. Left: Colourful hanging heliconia. Below: The delicate flower of the crepe ginger. Right: Lush tropical flora thrives in Mamiku Gardens.

The Day Sail

Boat or catamaran trips to Soufrière are a wonderful way to enjoy the highlights of the town, while avoiding the arduous drive along the west coast. The dramatic coastline is particularly spectacular when viewed from the sea and the vessels set sail from either Rodney Bay Marina in Gros Islet or the Vigie Marina in Castries. They sail close to the shore, providing glimpses of the quaint colourful fishing villages backed by granite cliffs. It is possible to opt for the "land and sea" version, which transports visitors in one direction by road and returns on the water. This provides an opportunity to see the incredible beauty along the west coast roads and to return relaxed and refreshed on the open water.

On arrival at Soufrière, visitors are transported by mini-bus to local attractions, such as the Diamond Mineral Baths, Botanical Gardens and Waterfall and the Sulphur Springs. Some itineraries include lunch at such spots as the Hummingbird Inn, the Soufrière Estate or more private venues. Other boats provide a picnic lunch back on board to allow more time for snorkelling on the way back up to Castries.

Detours into the idyllic harbour of Marigot Bay are usually included in the tour to allow visitors some time to relax and wander around in this "picture-perfect" setting.

There are boats of all descriptions available. The *Brig Unicorn* (452-8232) is a pirate ship in full sail and full of fun, while the *Vigie* (452-9423) is a motor yacht offering cool shade and comfort for the duration of the trip. Several catamarans also offer Soufrière trips, including the *Mango Tango* (452-8232), *Endless Summer* (Cats 450-8651) and *Carnival* (452-5586). Contact Mike Green at Cats if you are interested in chartering a catamaran for a private cruise.

For a private tour contact Captain Mike's (452-7044) or Mike Lagrenade (450-0705).

St. Lucia Helicopters

Pointe Seraphine
Telephone: 453-6950
Fax: 452-0298

This is sightseeing with a difference! The tropical landscape of St. Lucia takes on a whole new perspective from the air. Imagine skimming the tops of mountain ranges cloaked in dense trees before swooping down into the ravine in front of the bubbling Sulphur Springs. Fly above the towering trees of the rainforest, hover over sparkling waterfalls and skim across miles of banana

plantations. View the brightly painted villages, secret coves and the myriad flora from the air. The well-designed trips – giving visitors a choice of east or west coast – have a running commentary which provides some interesting and entertaining information about the landscape. The trip is costly, but provides a once-in-a-lifetime experience to witness the beauty of "Helen of the West Indies" from an unrivalled perspective.

Airport transfers are also available

Left: A catamaran moored at the spectacular snorkelling site of Anse Cochon on the west coast of St. Lucia. Above: The golden sands of Reduit Beach.

get

beached!

The beaches of St. Lucia come in all shapes, sizes and colours. Whatever their description, they all have two things in common – they are all beautiful and they are all free. There are no private beaches on the island. Fifty yards above high tide mark, around the entire coastline, is the Queen's Chain. This is public domain and it means that every single St. Lucian beach is yours to discover.

The north coast differs from the south, as do the beaches on the Atlantic. Some beaches offer calm and shallow waters, safe for infants, while others are wild, untamed and quite dangerous.

The busiest is **Reduit Beach** on the north-west coast. Three large resorts, the **Papillon,** the **Rex St. Lucian** and the **Royal St. Lucian,** are built along its shores as are as the **St. Lucia Yacht Club** and **Spinnakers' Bar and Restaurant.** People who live in the north of St. Lucia – and that is the majority of the population – flock here, especially at weekends. The sea is calm and safe and the sand is golden. Beach chairs and cold drinks are readily available

Main picture: The magnificent Reduit Beach sits on the north-west coast of St. Lucia. Right: Youngster braves the gentle surf!

and there is plenty to do. Sunfish sailing, windsurfing, waterskiing and jet skiing are all on offer here. Or you can simply sit back and let the world drift gently by.

At **Pigeon Island National Park** the beaches are small and fairly deserted, although facilities are good with freshwater showers, restrooms, restaurants and bars all within walking distance. As it is part of St. Lucia's National Parks system, a small fee is payable on entry.

The beach along the **Causeway** at Pigeon Island is one long stretch of uninterrupted sand that is free to the public. At weekends St. Lucians hold beach parties on the Causeway, but during the week it is fairly deserted until dusk when it is taken over by joggers.

The beach at **Le Sport Hotel** is an unusual blend of black and golden sand. Due to its proximity to the St. Lucia channel, where the Atlantic and Caribbean meet, the sea is chilly as it is constantly being refreshed by the cooler ocean's waters.

On the road leading to the **Windjammer Landing Resort,** an unmarked right-hand turning just before the hotel leads to **Trouya Beach.** This small but pleasant

strip of golden sand is where the inhabitants of the surrounding communities come to relax during the weekend.

The beach at Windjammer Landing is man-made with golden sand brought in from other parts of St. Lucia. The reef that runs parallel to the shore is a snorkelling paradise, particularly at the southern end of the beach near to the **East Winds Inn.**

Further along the main road at the Marisule traffic lights, a sharp right turn towards the sea leads to **Marisule Beach**. Residents always keep an ear out for the sound of a conch shell being blown. The low, honking noise carries across the neighbourhood as a signal that a catch of fish is waiting to be sold.

One long and particularly beautiful stretch of sand is **Vigie Beach**. It runs all the way from the airport right up to **Choc Bay**, beyond **Waves' Beach Bar**. Before the Gros Islet highway was built and opened up the northern sector of the island, Vigie Beach was the most fashionable place to bathe. Today, despite its central location, it remains more like a well-kept secret where there is plenty of room to stretch out and stroll. The sea is wonderfully clean and there is shade beneath the sea-almond trees where picnic tables have been erected.

It is the beach at **La Toc**, in front of **Sandals St. Lucia** that lures young dare-devils to surf during high seas. This beach is exposed to the northern breakers and is sometimes closed to swimmers as waves can be immense and the undertow extremely strong. Whenever the red flag is hoisted bathers know it is dangerous to swim. On calmer days, however, La Toc beach is a great place to the enjoy the day.

Marigot Bay is a yachtsman's haven. Made up of two bays, this is one of the most protected small harbours in St. Lucia. The inner bay is a refuge for yachts during bad weather. In the outer bay, near **Dolittles Restaurant**, there is a small, palm-fringed beach, on a spit of land.

Tour guides tell how the film *Dr. Dolittle*, starring Rex Harrison, was shot here. During shooting, freshwater tanks for the seals were installed in shady areas and banana trees were festooned with false flowers. The giant snail shell

Background: Grand Anse beach. Above: Local children are raised with a love of the sun and surf.

in which Dr. Dolittle sails away in the final sequence was left behind and served as a tourist attraction until it eventually fell apart.

There is no road access to Dolittles but, for a small fee, a little ferry carries people between the north and south shores. Dolittles offers food and drink and lots of action. Sunfish sailing and windsurfing are available, as well as plenty of underwater activities. Snorkelling is a popular pastime and there is an on-site Scuba diving operation.

One of the most frequented dive sites is found just south of Marigot Bay at **Anse Cochon**. This black sand beach is easily accessible from the sea. There are lots of fish to see in the shallow waters and experienced divers are taken out to the *Lesleen M*, a wreck sunk in 90 feet (28 metres) of water. The popularity of Anse Cochon means there are always plenty of boats bobbing off shore in the warm waters.

Further south, at **Anse Jambette**, Chef Harry, the owner of the Green Parrot, has built a small restaurant on this tiny sliver of black sand. Anse Jambette, just north of Canaries, is accessible by road or by sea and the small bay is safe for swimming and snorkelling.

In between Anse Jambette and Anse Chastanet to the north of Soufrière, there are many little coves to discover by boat. The sand along this stretch of coastline is predominately black, volcanic matter and glitters with microscopic grains of quartz. When the sun rises overhead the sand can reach sole-scorching temperatures, making the trip between beach towel and sea something of a sprint.

Anse Chastanet is bustling with activity. The majority of the boats within the bay belong to Scuba operations which come to dive at *Trou Diable*, part of Soufrière's marine park system. Anse Chastanet is a snorkellers' and Scuba divers' paradise and St. Lucia's PADI Five-Star Scuba St. Lucia is based here.

Less hectic beaches in Soufrière are at **Malgretoute** and **Jalousie** in between the Pitons. At Jalousie, the sea is a deep, navy blue. Once the shoreline starts to shelve away, it drops to depths as yet unfathomed. The sandy beach is fringed with coconut trees and a warm welcome awaits visitors looking for lunch at the **Jalousie Hilton**.

Above: Sunseekers relax on the golden sands of Reduit Beach. Below: Local teenages playing handball on Vigie Beach.

The sand is a warm gold and the sea, refreshed by the Atlantic, is salty and chilly, even during the hot summer months. Vieux Fort has a great horse riding tradition and St. Lucians love to gallop along the wide shores of the beach. Horses are often ridden bareback and sometimes without a bridle – the touch of a hand and the sound of a voice being sufficient to guide the animal.

The black pearl of Soufrière's beaches is **Anse l'Ivrogne.** Getting there by car requires an intimate knowledge of the un- marked and often unpaved road. However, the boat ride from the Soufrière jetty only takes members of the Soufrière Water Taxi Association five minutes.

Anse l'Ivrogne is magical. Nestled beneath the flanks of Gros Piton, the sea at the northern end of the beach is as deep and unfathomable as Jalousie. However, tucked away at the southern end is a sandy shoal

that extends no more than 75 feet (22 metres) into the sea. This provides an unexpected warm turquoise pool. Anse l'Ivrogne is nearly always deserted and a perfect place to enjoy solitude and tranquillity.

From Choiseul down to Laborie, there is a series of small beaches and coves to be explored. At **Laborie,** the black volcanic sand gives way to a warm gold.

The extreme southern coast of St. Lucia is all beach. **Anse de Sable** stretches from the outskirts of Vieux Fort town all the way round to the Atlantic shores beyond **Club Mediterranée**. This windswept shoreline is definitely one of the most beautiful places in St. Lucia.

Left: The deserted sands of Vigie Beach. Above: A perfect spot to relax in the sun! Right: St. Lucia offers visitors a host of watersports activities.

Seagrape trees line Anse de Sable and during the season, whole families descend on the area to pick the purple fruit that has a white pulp and a slightly bitter taste.

Maria Islands Nature Reserve faces Anse de Sable beach. It is home to one of the world's rarest creatures – the Maria Islands Ground Lizard. The Reserve can only be visited at certain times of the year. However, the little beach on Maria Island is a jewel. It is golden and sparkles with tiny pieces of quartz.

On the Atlantic coast, the beaches are wilder and sometimes difficult to access. On the extreme north Atlantic coast, **Donkey Beach** named after the herds of wild donkeys that used to live on the cactus-dotted slopes, is sandwiched between high cliffs which have been eroded by the sea and the wind. You need a four-wheel drive vehicle to reach this unexpected stretch of golden sand. The currents are treacherous and the sandy shelf drops off suddenly, leaving unsuspecting swimmers quite literally in deep water. This beautiful place is to be admired, but visitors should be circumspect in their approach to the pounding surf.

The same approach is recommended at all the wild Atlantic beaches such as **Grand Anse** near Babonneau, an impressive place that has a treacherous undertow; at **Louvet,** north of Au Leon, a majestic beach that is almost inaccessible except on foot; at **Honeymoon Beach**, north of Vieux Fort, a beautiful deserted place with deceptive undercurrents; and at **Fond d'Or** in Dennery, a wide, golden bay that is swept by the Atlantic

Background: Fabulous windswept beach on the east coast. Opposite: Moonlight sparkles on the sea at Smuggler's Cove. Above: Reduit Beach is ideal for families. Right: Golden sunset over the west coast of St. Lucia.

Ocean. Only the island's strongest surfers venture out into the breakers at Fond d'Or.

It is imperative that caution is exercised on the east coast beaches at all times, even if you are just walking in the surf. Visitors to this side of the island will witness a raw and natural beauty that should always be treated with respect.

There are a couple of safe Atlantic beaches to be found at **Cas en Bas**, near Gros Islet. Cas en Bas has a protected inner bay that is nearly always calm and therefore safe for swimming.

Comerette Point, to the south of Cas en Bas, is protected by a long peninsular and a series of reefs that make for safe bathing in the shallows. The beach is alternately sandy and pebbly and this long, varied piece of coastline is fascinating to explore. Access to Comerette Point is by four-wheel drive. The turn-off is on the Monchy road just before the community of La Feuillie.

Another sheltered Atlantic beach is located within the **Fregate Island Nature Reserve**. As this is part of an environmentally

sensitive area, access is only allowed with an authorised National Trust guide. Rather than being a constraint, this is probably the finest way to discover Fregate's unique flora and fauna, which only a knowledgeable guide can point out.

Whether you are looking for deserted stretches of black or white sand, beaches which buzz with action, wild and dangerous shores or calm and clear seas, look no further, St. Lucia can provide them all.

water world

The first pale blush of dawn brings lambent light to a scene of breathtaking beauty. Your boat rocks cradlelike on the water, the wind does not wake too early and the slight breeze gently slaps ropes against the mast inviting a melody of wind chimes. Otherwise silence is all around. As the minutes tick by, the dull blue sky lightens until the tip of the sun's golden rays pierce the horizon.

There is nothing so magical as waking up on a yacht. Some people find the cabins below confining and prefer to sleep on deck where they may be rewarded with the unique sensation of dawn at sea.

Day has come and the rising sun signals a rhythm change. The rigging clatters more actively against the mast as the wakened wind digs small furrows in the sea water. The early morning stillness is gone, an indication to go below and prepare breakfast.

This pre-dawn magic is just one reason why so many people come to the Caribbean to holiday on a chartered yacht. The lucky

Left: Lone yacht sails along the west shores of St. Lucia. Opposite: A graceful yacht makes its way towards the marina at Rodney Bay.

few even buy a boat so they can recapture those magical sensations more frequently.

Unless you have the means to purchase or charter an "Aristotle Onassis" style cruiser, you will find life on board a simple affair and generally without many of the comforts that are part of daily life ashore.

Galleys are small and compact and no space is wasted. There is no room for fine china, crystal or fancy cookware. Meals are simple and when yachties want to dine in style they go ashore. This avoids elaborate preparation and, better still, no washing up!

Freshwater is the most precious asset on board a boat so washing and even showering are done with a minimal amount of water. Toilets (called heads) use sea water.

Most chartered yachts have dining banquettes and tables below, but when the weather is fine (as it usually is in St. Lucia), the best place to eat is on deck.

Sleeping cabins are cosy little rooms placed at the fore and aft of the boat.

Despite the absence of many creature comforts, this simple life has great merit. With less time spent in the kitchen or worrying about what to wear (on-board wardrobes extend to bathing suits and casual clothing) there is more time to devote to sailing, swimming, snorkelling and serious relaxation.

St. Lucia is particularly well placed to cater to the yachting fraternity. It is the most central island in the Eastern Caribbean chain and is just a day's sail from St. Vincent and the Grenadines and a few sailing hours from Martinique. The island's own yachting attractions include beautiful anchorages and modern facilities.

The Caribbean coastline is the most accessible as the Atlantic tends to be rough and even the most sheltered bays are difficult and dangerous to navigate.

The best anchorages in the north of the island are at **Rodney Bay**. Yachties like to drop anchor off **Reduit Beach**, a sociable place to stay with its many bars and good restaurants. **The Causeway**, on the northern side of the bay, is a calm spot though some people choose to anchor closer to **Gros Islet**.

A convenient and secure anchorage is in the protected inner lagoon of Rodney Bay. The lagoon is dredged to 8-10 feet (2-3 metres) and is accessed through a man-made channel between Reduit Beach and the town of Gros Islet. The entrance is lit by port and starboards lights and by range lights that help when arriving at night.

The inner lagoon is home to the **Rodney Bay Marina** (VHF 16), the finest full service facility of its kind in the Eastern Caribbean. The marina is also an official port of entry into St. Lucia.

Rodney Bay Marina has 232 side-tie berths available at daily, monthly and long term rates. Some berths are for sale. Each has water and electricity (220 volts, 50 cycles) with transformers available for hire.

Wherever a yachtie decides to drop anchor, he must dispense with the entry formalities before anyone can disembark. At Rodney Bay, customs and immigration are located within the marina complex. Charges are quoted in EC$ and private yachts, depending on their length, pay between EC$30 and EC$40. There are additional charges for charter vessels. These standard rates are applicable at any of St. Lucia's ports of entry.

Rodney Bay Marina has a supermarket and liquor store, bakery and pharmacy, banks and

Above: The yachting haven of Marigot Bay is one of the safest anchorages in the Caribbean. Right: There is little that beats mooring a yacht in Rodney Bay and watch the golden sunset from the beach.

travel agency as well as some pleasant restaurants all located around a convivial courtyard. There are also hot showers and the marina provides garbage disposal services.

Rodney Bay Services, an ancillary of the marina, offers a same-day laundry service, ice and the refilling of propane gas cylinders. The company are very helpful and will put yachtsmen in touch with marine specialists who provide anything from mechanical to electrical services.

Rodney Bay Marina's dry dock (VHF 68), located on the northern side of the lagoon, is managed by some of the most experienced people in the yachting business.

The dry dock, the largest in St. Lucia, has a fifty-ton hoist and there is room for 150 yachts on long-term storage. There is an excellent duty-free chandlery, machine and paint shop, fibreglass repair facility and sail loft as well as GRP and mechanical workshop. Yachtsmen can do their repairs themselves or engage any one of the reputable companies that work in the marina.

For virtual access, Rodney Bay Marina's website address is www.rodneybaymarina.com

Yacht charter organisations within the marina include **Destination St. Lucia** (DSL) that specialises in bareboat charters – the name used to describe yacht rentals with no crew or provisioning provided. DSL has a fleet of yachts, the largest of which is 51 feet (16 metres).

DSL also provides long term maintenance, repair and baby-sitting services for private yachts. Their foreign language service translates German, Portuguese, English, French, Italian and Russian.

Further south, **Marigot Bay** one of the most secluded and safest anchorages in the Caribbean, is another yachting attraction. It is also an official port of entry. Like all St. Lucian ports, Marigot has seen its fair share of historical events.

This sheltered bay is one mile (1.6km) south of the Hess Oil depot at Cul de Sac, a conspicuous landmark especially at night as it is always brightly lit. The entrance to Marigot is easily identified. Yachtsmen need to look out for a house with a red roof, perched high on a cliff at the southern entrance.

Yachts are advised to stay on the southern side of the channel and to anchor in the inner harbour where holding is fair in soft mud.

St. Lucia's biggest yacht charter company is based in Marigot. **Moorings Yacht Charters,** monitors VHF 16 and 25 and specialises in long distance and day charters. Their thirty-five boat fleet includes Beneteau 39's and Morgan 60's. They offer both bareboat and crewed charters and take care of all provisioning.

The small marina at Marigot offers long and short term docking. The twenty-six slips can accommodate yachts up to 200 feet (61 metres) in length while the Moorings takes care of fuel, water and ice needs. There is a mechanic shop, sail loft, laundry, mini-market and garbage disposal facilities.

The Moorings also manages the **Hurricane Hole Hotel**. This small resort is made up of sixteen cottages set in a Caribbean garden. Central facilities include a bar, restaurant and pool.

Soufrière is the most spectacular anchorage in St. Lucia. The most popular places to drop anchor include Anse Chastanet – home of a first-class hotel of the same name; the Hummingbird Inn – slightly north of the town and a lively bar and restaurant; Malgretoute to the north of Petit Piton and Jalousie Bay directly between the Pitons.

Soufrière is an official port of entry and the town's entire coastal zone is a Marine Reserve. All yachts anchoring within the area must purchase a Coral Conservation Permit from the **Soufrière Marine Management Authority** (Tel: 459-5500) located near Soufrière's main jetty. The cost depends on the size of the vessel and the length of stay.

Mooring buoys have been installed for yachts. As this entire area is home to the most pristine reefs in St. Lucia, it is strictly forbidden to throw out anchors within the marine reserve. In fishing priority areas, yachtsmen must give way to fishermen.

Above and below: St. Lucia offers yachtsmen a host of perfect moorings in tropical surroundings.

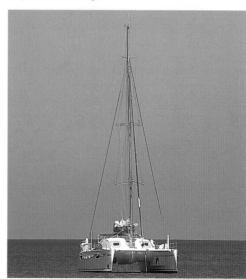

Fishing priority areas are Roseau Bay, the north eastern corner of Soufrière Bay, the north and southern flanks of Malgretoute, the inner Jalousie Bay (Anse des Pitons) and Anse L'Ivrogne.

Other protected marine areas include mangroves, beaches, coral and artificial reefs and fishing priority areas. It is forbidden to dump garbage and flush toilets less than one mile from shore. It is illegal to buy, sell or collect coral. Heavy fines are imposed when people are caught buying lobsters outside of the official season which runs from September 1st to April 30th. Spear gun fishing is strictly illegal, though trawling a line to catch dinner is allowed.

Diving is forbidden within the Marine Reserves unless accompanied by a licensed dive operator or guide recommended by the Soufrière Marine Management Authority. Dive permits must also be purchased.

Another excellent innovation in Soufrière is the local Water Taxi Association created in 1996 by a group of small craft owners who felt that yachtsmen and tourists were being hassled by boat boys.

The Association provides ship-to-shore transportation, shopping expeditions and airport transfers to Vigie Airport just thirty-five minutes away. The Association's members also specialise in snorkelling trips to Anse Chastanet, Jalousie, Anse L'Ivrogne and Malgretoute. The water taxis are licensed and insured. They carry all the necessary safety equipment and their covered decks provide welcome shade. Tariffs are standard and water taxis are the best way to avoid the discomfort of the bumpy Soufrière roads and enjoy St. Lucia's most spectacular stretch of coastline.

The Association's membership also includes boat boy services.

The boat boys are not permitted to carry passengers, but for a set fee, will tie off stern lines and organise beach barbecues. Another handy service is the supply of boat watchman while yachties vacate their vessel for lunch or dinner ashore.

Both the Soufrière Water Taxi Association and the Soufrière Marine Management Authority monitor VHF 16.

Castries Harbour, far less picturesque than Soufrière, is a convenient anchorage, centrally located near the main administrative and shopping centres of the capital. Vessels entering Castries Harbour need to avoid the shoal that extends to the west of Tapion Peak. The lighthouse on Vigie Hill, at the mouth of the port, flashes twice every ten seconds. While Castries Harbour is an official entry point, it is also one of the busiest ports in the Caribbean. It is, therefore, much easier for yachtsmen to clear immigration and customs formalities through Rodney Bay.

Nearby **Vigie Creek** is a more secluded anchorage where repair facilities and food supplies are available. **St. Lucia Yacht Services** at Vigie Marina (VHF 16) provides water, fuel, electricity and car rentals. The company also has up to twenty berths available. During certain months, a strong surge makes docking at the Vigie Marina almost impossible.

St. Lucia's second dry dock facility is located on the northern shore just outside the port. **Castries Yacht Centre** sells fuel, has a thirty-five ton travel lift, chandlery, tool rental centre, canteen and laundry.

Anse Cochon is three miles south of Marigot Bay. This bay, along with Anse Galet to the north, is part of the Marine Reserve. This makes Anse Cochon one of the best places to snorkel and scuba dive. However, the bay tends to get busy with dive operators and day charter vessels. It is also a fishing priority area.

Vieux Fort is probably the least exploited of all of St. Lucian anchorages. However that will change once a planned marina is completed. The best place to drop anchor is off the main harbour or below the Kimitrai Hotel. Vieux Fort, St. Lucia's second town, is an official port of entry and boats can clear customs and immigration at the docks. Vieux Fort is St. Lucia's southernmost port of call. For southbound vessels, the next stop is St. Vincent.

For people who just want a quick taste of St. Lucia's coastline, a day excursion is the best option. One of the most experienced boats offering day excursions is the private yacht Vigie. This 56-foot (17-metre) motor cruiser specialises in all types of day trips that take in the coastline from Pigeon Island to the Pitons.

The *Brig Unicorn* is a 140-foot replica of a 19th-century brigantine and was used in the television series *Roots*. It offers a land and sea tour to Soufrière, the Sulphur Springs, Diamond Falls and the Botanical Gardens. An on-board buffet lunch, is provided. Snorkelling and swimming at Anse Cochon as well as a quick visit to Marigot Bay are included in the trip. The *Brig Unicorn* also offers moonlight and sunset cruises.

The elegant, 56-foot (17-metre) *Endless Summer* catamarans offer almost the same itinerary as the *Brig Unicorn*. The party ambience on *Endless Summer* and the *Brig Unicorn* is fuelled by plenty of rum punch and lively music.

Several other companies provide day boat charters for smaller groups. With **Hackshaw's Boat Charters**, the oldest boat charter company in St. Lucia, customers can design their own day at sea. **Douglas' Sailing Tours** will take clients anywhere they want to go, including Martinique.

Opposite: Rodney Bay. Centre: Marigot Bay is a lively anchorage with a choice of restaurants and bars. Below: Anse Chastanet is an idyllic mooring.

underwater

extravaganza

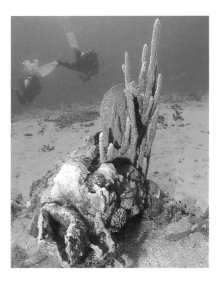

Thrusting precipitously from the azure waters of Soufrière Bay, the Piton Mountains soar, their base truncated by a line of deepest blue. Now imagine these majestic peaks in mirror image, by continuing down below the surface of the sea. Beneath the clear waters is a terrace that surrounds the Pitons like the brim of a witch's hat. This quickly changes back to the very steep slopes, walls and cliffs that are so characteristic of these volcanic plugs. There is life everywhere – it seems that every crevice is filled and every opportunity for colonisation taken with life living upon life, beside it, or within it. This is what diving in St. Lucia is all about – the incredible diversity of fish, invertebrates and corals.

The calm waters of the Caribbean combined with the steeply-sloping dive sites provide perfect conditions for a multitude of hard and soft corals, sponges and gorgonians. In turn, these diverse life forms create the necessary places for an extensive variety of fish and invertebrate species to co-exist. The combination has

Left: St. Lucia is home to a fantastic and diverse array of marine life. Above: The waters of the Caribbean provide perfect conditions for hard and soft corals.

provided one of the most colourful and interesting dive locations anywhere in the Caribbean. For the photographer and videographer, clear water and plentiful marine life offer the possibility of great shots and footage. For the fish watcher there is a chance to see many different, and often rare, species interacting. For those who simply enjoy diving the varied terrain offers a host of underwater gardens to see and explore.

There are two main dive areas in St. Lucia, both on the Caribbean coastline. Anse Cochon provides sites reasonably close to Castries and the hotels in the north. Further south is the best-known dive area on the island which is known as Anse Chastanet.

There are other sites, both in the north and Vieux-Fort areas, but they are not well visited, even though diving can be extremely good. St. Lucia had no marine reserves until quite recently. First on the scene were a pair of shipwrecks, not specifically sunk to provide diving, although that was the result. The original aim was to create artificial reefs to attract fish. More recently the creation of the **Soufrière Marine Management Area** has seen a community-based attempt to find

common ground between all the user groups and to thereby protect this unique environment.

THE SOUFRIÈRE MARINE MANAGEMENT AREA

Conflicting demands upon the resources around Soufrière were turning the normally tranquil waters into stormy seas as fishermen, yachtsmen, divers and other marine users vied for territorial supremacy. To ease these problems the Soufrière Marine Management Area was conceived, and, over a period of eighteen months, meetings were held to harmonise the needs of the interested parties. The waters from Anse L'Ivrogne to the south of Gros Piton northward to Anse Mamin were divided into areas, some assigned as marine reserves, others allowed fishing or the mooring of yachts, while the balance were designated as multipurpose areas where

everyone could enjoy the waters. There were teething problems but in general the concept has worked extremely well. The rules of the SMMA and the area designations have been modified as the needs of the user groups changed but overall tranquillity has returned to the waters of Soufrière. For further information contact the SMMA Office on Bay Street, Soufrière. Tel: 459-5500. e-mail: smma@candw.lc

THE SOUFRIÈRE AREA

Anse Chastanet

By far the best-known dive location on St. Lucia, the Anse Chastanet area comprise of wonderfully diverse dive sites. There are coral gardens teeming with reef fish and beds of sea grass that are home to a multitude of marine creatures. Within a few fin strokes you can find yourself at the lip of a

Top: Colourful sea slug. Centre: Delicate Christmas tree tube worm. Top right: Dainty angel fish. Right: Exploring the myriad wonders of the magnificent reefs of St. Lucia.

vertiginous drop that plunges deep into the abyss, or you may find yourself peering into the inky darkness of small caves and caverns. If there is such a thing as a single dive area that satisfies everyone, this must be it.

Turtle Reef

Turtle Reef is a crescent located in the centre of Anse Chastanet Bay, and the most northern dive site in the area. Set offshore about 110 yards (100 metres), it ranges in depth from about 30 feet (9 metres) to well over 170 feet (50 metres). On the outermost side the coral falls away rapidly. There is often a current running north to south which can be strong. In addition to the coral, the sea grass beds inshore of the reef often turn up some very interesting creatures such as migrating seahorses during the summer months. Flying gurnard are often seen along with hawksbill turtles and very occasionally eagle rays. For those with patience and good eyesight

many fascinating creatures can be found in the grass. Look for decorator crabs, the small but ferocious yellowface pikeblenny, rosy razor fish that can bury themselves in the sand in the blink of an eye, urchins and many others. On the main reef, large shoals of grunts can be found, usually in the back of the crescent and on top of the reef. On occasion, large shoals of southern sennet visit this same area, while numerous crustaceans hide in the many crevices of the reef. On the seaward side of the reef, a shoal of margate can to be found at about 60 feet (18 metres). If you have a sharp eye, you might also find a frog fish or two, blending perfectly with the sponges they call home. Though small, this reef is extremely well populated and should be taken slowly for full appreciation.

Anse Chastanet Reef

This reef has to be one of the best shore dives anywhere. Simply walk into the water and within a few seconds, you will be swimming amongst coral and surrounded by curious Bermuda chubb, sergeant majors and many other fish looking for food. A few more strokes and the reef falls away in a series of steep slopes with terraces in between. Depths ranges from 10 feet to over 330 feet (3 metres to over 100 metres).

The reef is superb at all depths of normal sport diving, whether just below the surface or at 130 feet (39 metres). As you sink from the top of the reef at about 12 feet (4 metres) the first terrace can be seen sloping down to about 33 feet (10 metres). The reef then falls rapidly to 60 feet (18 metres), where it levels off for a short distance, and then drops again to over 100 feet (30 metres). In addition there are several fingers of sand that cut back into the reef creating overhangs and walls. In the shallows there is a large cavern and several small caves. The shallow reef is mostly composed of boulder coral like star, finger and brain coral with some fire coral and a little stag and elk horn coral. As you go deeper this changes to leaf, plate and sheet coral. There are more than twenty five different species on this reef. In general the fish here enjoy good protection and tend to be a little larger and more inquisitive than will be seen elsewhere. It is not uncommon to see large solitary barracuda, and numerous jacks. At times the front of the cavern is teeming with silversides and other baitfish, shoals so dense that they resemble a pool of mercury. At the far end of this dive site, in the late afternoon, shoals of boga and other small fish can be seen being aggravated by black jacks, bar jacks, horse-eye jacks and rainbow runners. In fact, virtually every reef fish included in any Caribbean fish identification guides can be found on this reef,

so diverse is its population. There can be strong currents which are extremely deceptive in this area. The combination of clear water and steep slopes makes it easy to misjudge your depth, so exercise caution.

Fairyland Wall

This site is located at the outer end of the Anse Chastanet Reef dive. It is a deeper dive and needs boat cover. It starts at about 60 feet (18 metres) and drops away as a wall to over 330 feet (100 metres). It is best to start at 130 feet (39 metres) gradually moving into shallower water as you head back towards the shore. The last part follows the Anse Chastanet shore dive in reverse. The advantage is that you get to see some of the larger fish that inhabit these waters. It is here that the most aggressive feeding takes place if conditions are right. In addition this is a superb wall with lots of black coral. As with all the dives in this area, currents can be

strong. If a current is felt at the start of the dive, you should make your way down to the drop off as quickly as possible, then keep well below the lip of the drop off avoiding the current's effects.

Fairyland

As the name suggests this is a magical place. It can be dived in a number of ways, as a shallow dive in the 40 feet (12 metres) range, or as a medium dive at up to about 60 feet (18 metres). It can be dived north to south or vice-versa. The normal start point is from a boat, at the base of the headland in Anse Chastanet Bay. You then head south across the Grand Caille headland until you meet a coral covered rock outcrop that reaches very close to the surface. Once here, you move out to sea and round this outcrop to find numerous routes to cross this gently sloping, shallow area. Once you arrive at the far side you will find another coral outcrop, which again reaches to just below the surface. Circle this outcrop in either direction – mostly to the right – out to the

point and around. On the far side there is a fairly narrow terrace which drops away as a wall. *(See Grand Caille dive site below)*. If you go left on arriving at the outcrop you will find yourself gradually getting shallower and moving from sand pool to sand pool over coral ridges. The currents on this dive can be strong, so test the waters before you go. They can also be quite unpredictable so boat cover is essential. That apart, Fairyland is one of the prettiest dives in the Caribbean. The currents are responsible for the large shoals of horseye jacks that can be seen, not to mention the silversides which they feed on. There is often a shoal of squid in the shallows close to the headland. They are a delight to watch as they dance just below the surface.

Grand Caille (The Big House)

This dive on the far side of the Grand Caille Headland starts close to a small beach called Trou Diable. The dive is made from this area back towards the point of the Grand Caille headland. It starts at about 40 feet (12

metres) on a terrace and moves out to the lip of a steep slope running down and away from the shore. Following the lip, the steep slope turns into a wall, with the lip at about 50 feet (15 metres). The dive progresses along the wall and ends by returning up the wall, over the lip and into the shallows in the same area that the Fairyland dive often ends. Try to always stay close to the wall as there can be strong downward currents away from

Opposite: Scuba diver amidst a host of brightly-coloured reef fish. Above: There are many wrecks worth diving in the waters off St. Lucia where the vessels are encrusted with marine life. Below: Dazzling finger coral is prolific around Anse Chastanet.

the wall, and it is possible to drift deeper than you planned. This is a great dive, with abundant fish and coral.

DIVE SITES BETWEEN THE GRAND CAILLE AND SOUFRIÈRE

Trou Diable (The Devil's Hole)

This site is named after the cauldron-like effect the boulders create in bad weather. This is an excellent second dive and takes in numerous massive coral covered boulders. They lie together and form many small caverns and passageways where fish love to hide. There is no set route on this shallow dive as most of the instructors have their own way of tackling it, and they are all good. Take time to look into every nook and cranny – some are large enough to swim into. They teem with interesting reef fish, including large puffer fish, shoals of copper sweepers and masses of grunts.

Pinnacles

This is a spectacular site that consists of four pinnacles which thrust almost to the surface. The

Background: Colourful reef fish make their home among the rocks and reefs of St. Lucia. Centre: Scuba diver examines a coral covered boulder. Opposite top: Stunning coral formations are found in all shapes, colours and sizes. Opposite: Exquisite anenomes abound on the coral reef.

site is sometimes referred to as the **Keyhole Pinnacles**, because of a cut-out through the cliff above the dive site, which resembles a keyhole. The dive starts on the Soufrière side of this keyhole, the bottom is only 40 feet (12 metres) at this point, but it slopes away quickly and 50 feet (15 metres) is reached by the time you encounter the first small pinnacle. As you pass it the next two appear standing side by side. These have their base at 60 feet (18 metres) and the larger pinnacle clears the surface in a big swell. The main part of the dive should be spent circling these marvels of nature that look distinctly like miniature versions of the Pitons. The last pinnacle appears just as you are losing sight of the previous two. It is also very large and worth circumnavigating before ending the dive. The most common coral at the base of the pinnacles is finger coral. Huge beds of this delicate and very beautiful coral extend down from the pinnacles which are also host

to numerous other corals. Seahorses can be seen clinging to the branches of gorgonian coral. Divers have to be particularly attentive to spot them for they turn their backs away from "predators" blending perfectly with their surroundings.

Hummingbird Wall

This site, close to the Still and Hummingbird restaurants, is not often dived as the coral is in poor condition due to silting and fresh water from the Soufrière River. However, it is a fun dive close to the beach. Look for warm sulphurous bubbles percolating out of the sand, providing further evidence of the islands volcanic origins. The wall itself is deeply convoluted, with numerous peep-holes that are densely covered with sea whips.

THE PITON AREA

Malgretoute (Despite All)

The area just to the north of Petit Piton was once a leper colony but now a gorgeous black sand beach lined with stately palms denotes the starting

point of this site. It is best dived at about 60 feet (18 metres) or less. Enter the water at the Piton end of the beach and simply make your way towards the Pitons point. Sandy patches soon lead to solid coral on a very steep slope of about forty-five degrees. The slope remains fairly constant for most of the dive. Worth noting are the massive barrel sponges that can be seen on this and most of the dives here. Shoals of fish, southern sennet, jacks, creole wrasse and grunts pass through the area and the site boasts plenty of reef fish.

Superman's Flight

This dive is a continuation of Malgretoute, and for the most part the terrain is similar. There is however a small wall in the shallows at the end of the dive which is covered in gorgonians. Large seahorses have been seen amongst the coral from time to time. This site was originally named after a scene in the film *Superman II* and was indeed well named as the currents here are amongst the strangest of any in St. Lucia. It is possible to see divers gliding along with the

current going north at 60 feet (18 metres) while above them at 30 feet (10 metres) another group drift south. Do not let this deter you – it adds to the fun and colour of the dive. The strange currents attract many species of fish, along with their predators.

The Piton Wall

This dive starts in the gouge left by a massive landslide on the Petit Piton. It is best made as a deep dive of close to 130 feet (39 metres). You enter the water, drop down the gouge and head seaward once at depth. You will quickly encounter the wall which reputedly falls to about 1,000 feet (300 metres). This is the most dramatic of St. Lucia's wall dives and it is covered in spectacular corals, sponges and gorgonians, and there are plenty of fish. As you

move into the shallows at the end of the dive there is a gently sloping ledge at about 30 feet (10 metres) where divers occasionally encounter the ghostly yellowhead jawfish. They can be seen hovering inches above their burrows in the sand. Approach slowly or they will back down out of sight. They are sometimes seen with their open mouth full of eggs. Males hatch them by keeping them in their mouths for about fourteen days.

Jalousie and Gros Piton Dive Sites

These two excellent sites are grouped together because they are similar in many ways. Jalousie starts close to *Bang between the Pitons*, Lord Glenconner's unique waterfront restaurant and ends at a light coloured triangular cliff at the centre of Gros Piton. This is also the start of the Gros Piton dive site, which continues towards the point. Both dives take place on a slope of about forty-five degrees and the bottom is mainly rubble covered with corals, gorgonians

and massive barrel sponges. Fish are abundant and diverse and the current is generally just strong enough to make finning unnecessary. There are times however when both sites can be included in a single dive if the current is being hyperactive. This creates an exciting dive but it makes close-up photography virtually impossible. It is preferable to concentrate on video or wide-angle photography anywhere on the Piton sites. In general these dives are best undertaken at about 40 to 60 feet (15 to 18 metres). The coral does extend deeper but is often interspersed with sand.

Gros Piton Point

This site is rarely visited yet it is an excellent dive. It is best made at about 80 feet (27 metres) but first check on the direction of the current before committing to one direction or another. The point is made up of terraces which drop even deeper. The corals are more sparse than other sites with lots of sand patches, though southern stingrays are often seen in the area, along with turtles and the rare sargassum triggerfish which make this dive a worthwhile experience. They are numerous and fascinating,

and hover just above sponges as they watch divers warily. When approached, their silver eyelids flash provocatively before they slip down inside their favourite sponge to hide.

The Blue Hole of Anse L'Ivrogne

This site is rarely visited. It sustained severe storm damage a few years ago and the corals have been slow to recover. However it is an exciting deep dive, with a very unusual entry. The site gets its name because when viewed from above, there appears to be a hole in the ocean floor. In fact the sand drops away so fast that if a dive boat is tied with its bow on shore you can drop into almost 100 feet (30 metres) at the boat's stern. Dropping down this perilously steep sand wall is a strange experience, but once at depth you can make your way out to a convoluted rock and coral wall.

ANSE COCHON AREA
Anse Galet (Jellyfish Bay)

This dive starts on the Anse Galet Beach. Take care here as the poisonous *fer de lance* snake inhabits the area. The site is made up of a series of coral covered rock fingers that extend from just a few

feet below the surface to about 50 feet (15 metres). Divers generally weave in and out of the fingers as they slowly head towards the point.

Anse La Raye Wall

Starting on the northern side of the point, this is the best coral dive in the area. It mostly consists of large coral-covered boulders,but is also home to numerous fish and the occasional turtle. There is even a small wall area that drops from the surface to between 30 and 40 feet (10 and 13 metres). There are many places for marine life to hide so take the time to peep into every hole. Once you have rounded the point, the bottom shallows and eventually you find yourself on a small beach.

Opposite: St. Lucia is home to fantastic corals. Below: Colourful sea anenome.

There are shoals of grunts and soldier fish towards the bottom at the bow and stern. Currents here can be vicious, so if you experience problems, stay close to the wreck and work your way around to the leeward side.

The *Daini Koyomaru* Wreck

This most recent addition to the wrecks of St. Lucia was sunk in September 1996 at the southern end of Anse Cochon. She lies in 110 feet (33 metres) of water, and is a 16,000 ton dredger that had been use to clear Vieux-Fort

Anse Cochon (Pig's Bay)

This is an excellent first dive. You can begin at standing depth on the beach which has some coral at the northern end. Simply follow the sand coral interface and head out. The water gradually gets deeper reaching about 50 feet (15 metres) at the point. The coral becomes prolific further from the beach and eventually covers the bottom as well. There is a wide variety of reef fish and other marine life and for the most part visibility is good. Currents are generally light to non-existent.

Above: The rich diversity of nature is displayed with spectacular effect on the coral reef. Centre: Seahorses can be found on the Lesleen "M" Wreck. Opposite: Anse La Raye wall reveals some of the best coral in St. Lucia. Opposite top: The endangered hawsbill turtle.

The *Lesleen "M"* Wreck

This wreck was sunk in the Anse Cochon area in 1985 as an artificial reef. She was 165 foot (48 metre) coastal freighter, which amongst other things carried cement. She now rests at a maximum of 70 feet (21 metres) on an even keel. The stern section is well encrusted with corals and sponges, not to mention hydroids, so be careful not to touch as they cause a burning sensation on contact with skin. There are many areas where it is possible to penetrate the wreck, but be warned she is extremely fragile, and even exhaled bubbles can bring parts, not to mention silt, slipping down. Eel, octopus and seahorses are in residence and stingrays are sometimes seen.

harbour. At 244 feet (64 metres), it is the largest and most easily accessible wreck on the island. Much of its interior was left untouched and provides plenty of places for exploration. The wreck is already well-encrusted with life, particularly its bottom, which was covered in coral when the vessel was still in use. The wreck lies on its side and consequently these corals were not disturbed when it was sunk and continue to thrive. Currents can be strong, so keep to the leeward side.

OTHER DIVE LOCATIONS

Wawinet Wreck

This is possibly the best wreck dive in St. Lucia. The wreck was sunk near Moule-à-Chique in the 1980s to act as a FAD (Fish Attraction Device). The wreck is often surrounded by large shoals of grunts and soldier fish, with pelagics guarding the perimeter. She is a large wreck, 360 feet (110 metres) in length,

and lies on her starboard side in about 110 feet (33 metres) of water. The area is prone to very strong currents so this is not a dive for either the novice or inexperienced. Make your way down to the wreck as quickly as possible. Once there you will be treated to the sight of her superstructure and masts leaning over the sand. The dive is short because of the depth involved.

Shark Point

This area, close to Moule-à-Chique, is sadly rarely dived these days. There is good diving here, although there is not as much solid coral cover as Soufrière. The terrain is interesting and sightings of large pelagic fish are quite common. The bottom ranges from small walls to gentle slopes with many variations in between. Queen triggerfish are common in this area.

Barrel of Beef

The Barrel of Beef is a rocky outcrop which lies to the north of Labrelotte Bay, just south of Pigeon Island and opposite Rodney Bay. It is a small site used by the northern dive operators whenever the weather is unsuitable for the longer trip to the south of the island. Circumnavigation of the rock takes about thirty-five minutes. The bottom is made up of sloping rock covered by many soft corals. The visibility tends to be somewhat less tham further south and the fish life is sparse.

flora

fiesta

Mountains towering in a skyline outlined against the intense cobalt of the Caribbean sky and draped in a cloak of flowing greens with gently folding valleys and plunging ravines – this is the perfect setting for the spectacular floral spectrum which blooms year round on St. Lucia. The native blossoms are limitless, with some endemic species as timeless as the mountains themselves. Others are more recent imports and reflect the heritage of the various peoples who have carved out this enchanted island's history.

The centre portion of the island supports ancient trees of the rainforest dripping with various liana and is bordered by spreading fans of the shady tree fern. The general forests of lower elevations boast myriad trees and shrubs, which provide a safe haven for the birdlife of the island. They are also the source of many local remedies for ailments of heart, body and soul. The rugged Atlantic coastline demonstrates the harsh conditions survived only by hardy vegetation, yet is bordered by life-sustaining mangroves. So much diversification of foliage on only 248 square miles (640 sq km) makes St. Lucia the nature lover's treasure trove, just waiting to be discovered and shared.

Many of the most vivid floral species found in St. Lucia are those which have come from other lands. As world travel became a reality after Columbus' first voyage, a constant exchange of cultures began, including an influx of vegetation, either for food or aesthetic purposes.

For example, the tall **breadfruit tree**, with its large fingered leaves and green globes of fruit, was the very cause of Captain Bligh's mutiny. Young breadfruit saplings were his main cargo during his fateful voyage. History suggests that the final act that spurred the mutiny was when Bligh ordered for the saplings to be doused with the meagre supply of water that was meant for the crew. He did manage, however, to transport this staple starch crop intended to help feed the growing slave population in a subsequent voyage to the region.

Today, a popular dish is created by boiling, mashing and refrying the breadfruit's cream-coloured pulp into balls.

The most common flower of the Caribbean is the hibiscus, with over 200 known species and a grand range of colours: red, pink, yellow, orange, white and colour-fringed hybrids. It is a common ornamental garden plant with large, unmistakable flowers which bloom for only a day. Many varieties are present in almost every garden of the region from the sprawling grounds of the grand hotels to the manicured and cultured displays at the Diamond Falls and Botanical Gardens in Soufrière and Mamiku Gardens in Mon Repos.

Originating in the South Pacific, the trumpet-shaped flowers have four to five petals, creating the

Top left: The ostrich ginger plume is a native of Malaysia. Top right and bottom left: The hibiscus is a symbol of the tropics. Bottom right: Spectacular orchids are a common sight in St. Lucia. Above: The magnificent flamboyant originates in Madagascar.

medium hardness and is often used in furniture, due to its distinct blond colour streaked in blue-grey. The wood also has a unique ability to hold water and is often carved into flower vases.

base for the characteristically long stamen tube. The hibiscus has become so popular throughout the area it is almost synonymous with the word "tropical". The double varieties, with two sets of petals, can resemble a rose from a distance. The most distinguished and species is the coral hibiscus. Its delicate lacy petals curl upward, while the protruding stamen tube hangs several inches below.

The **tree hibiscus**, or **blue mahoe,** originates in Hawaii, but has been cultivated in St. Lucia in recent years by the Forestry Department. The blossom is a tightly woven hibiscus flower that blooms in brilliant yellow. As the day progresses the flower gradually darkens to orange and then bronze before dropping to the ground. The wood of the hibiscus tree is of

Top: The ginger lily is a plant which bears a spike of waxy red bracts. Right: The hibiscus is a beautiful garden plant whose unmistakable flowers bloom for only a day. Centre: The dazzling ixora is a common sight in St. Lucia. Opposite: The allamanda is an ornamental shrub with golden yellow funnel-shaped flowers.

Another popular garden flower with roots reaching outside the Caribbean is the **ginger lily**. A native of sout-east Asia, its broad leaves provide an attractive foliage throughout the year. The large waxy bracts form a plume (hence the plant's other name, the "ostrich plume"). Tiny white flowers are barely visible just inside the bracts. In fact, most people believe that the brilliant red bracts are the flower.

This is typical of many tropical plants. A different part of the plant – either the bract or leaves – provide the vibrant colours to attract pollinating birds and insects to the inconspicuous blossoms. The **poinsettia**, a native of Mexico, which, in its natural habitat of the tropics, can reach up to 12 feet

(4 metres) in height, is a good example. It is the leaves that turn bright red or white surrounding minute yellow flowers.

Superman, who swept between the twin peaks of the Pitons in Soufrière to land beside the cascading waterfall in the film *Superman II,* plucked the exotic "bird of paradise" for Lois Lane. Again, not from this region, but from Africa, this most unusual flower is found in most hotel and botanical gardens. The huge stalk bends horizontally and develops a bluish-grey sheath, from which the three sepals rise in flaming orange like out-stretched wings. The male portion of the flower juts forward in a contrasting bluish-purple to resemble the head and protruding neck of this elegant bird.

From the Far East comes the **ixora,** a small bush of dark green, shiny ovate leaves. The small individual flowers of four petals bloom in small clusters, forming a "flower ball" similar to that of a snowball in

flaming tropical colours. Red is the most common, but the ixora is also seen in yellow, pink and white.

Providing borders and hedges for almost every property on the island is the profusion of colour from the **bougainvillaea.** This climbing, thorny shrub often forms hedges and comes in a grand assortment of colours, including purple, magenta, orange, pink, rose, white and mixed combinations. The dazzling sprays of this symbol of the tropics actually consist of bracts – the flowers being small, white and tubular in shape.

Mystery shrouds the ancient, white trumpets of the **datura,** or **angel's trumpet**. The intoxicating, scent emitted by the elongated bell-shaped flowers – which can stretch to 10 inches (25 cm) on larger bushes are suggestive of the strong narcotic influence of this deadly plant. The datura originates in Central America, where ancient tribes

were known to drink its milk during sacred rites. The potent mixture was only served to highest members of the tribe's religious hierarchy. Often, these high priests were elevated to positions as messengers of the gods because the narcotic caused irreversible brain damage, and in many cases, even death.

The **heliconia** species, many of which are native to this region, are extremely varied and are among the most popular floral exhibits in most hotels and botanical gardens. They require the tropical conditions of warmth and humidity for growth. Each individual species is unique in shape and vividly coloured – usually in rich reds, oranges and yellows. They are members of the same family as the cultivated banana plant and have similar broad, paddle-shaped leaves. The bracts form intriguing shapes, such as sprouting spikes or dangling claws.

popular trees of St. Lucia is the **flamboyant,** or **poinciana.** The spreading limbs form a perfect umbrella for sweltering summer days and an elegant backdrop for the fiery red blossoms. Each flower consists of five petals, one of which is whitish-yellow streaked in crimson. Although red is the most common colour, some trees sport flowers of yellow or orange. As the blooms wither and fall, so do the feather-like leaves, leaving behind long black pods, which blow in the wind with an odd "*chak-a-ty-chak*" sound.

Flower-bearing bushes are limitless. In addition to rich colour, island gardens always include species which may be subtle in appearance but are mesmerising in scent. The creamy-white flowers of the **honeysuckle** always add a gentle, seductive fragrance to any garden. Their perfume, however, is diminished against that of the **jasmine.** With its delicate white flowers and dark green leaves, this native of China produces an aroma which hangs heavy in the night air. When mixed with the gentle Caribbean trade winds and the glow of a full moon, the heady fragrance creates the perfect ambience for your most sensuous St. Lucian memories.

The island has three varieties of the towering **cedar tree**. Its delicate trumpet-shaped flowers grow in clusters and begin to appear shortly after the dry season in March. A few months later the blossoms fall, laying a carpet of petals across the ground below. In full bloom, a tall yellow cedar, or *poui*, is one of the most stunning trees of the island.

While strolling through gardens, parks or forest, note that the canopy overhead is as diverse in colour, fragrance and form as the flowering shrubs. One of the most

Originating in Central America, the **frangipani** or **pagoda tree** forms a broad spread of branches from which the fragrant five-petal blossoms emerge. The colour combinations are limitless, ranging from delicate pink to subdued yellow, from brilliant red to the island's own indigenous white variety.

Background: The vibrant bougainvillea is common throughout St. Lucia. Above: The fragrant flowers of the frangipani. Centre: Delicate orchid in Mamiku Gardens.

This tree does surprisingly well in drier areas of St. Lucia, such as the extreme northern and southern ends and the Atlantic coastline. If the climate is particularly harsh, the tree will drop its leaves to conserve the moisture needed for the ambrosial flowers.

As the name suggests, the **African tulip tree** is a transplant that produces circular clusters of brilliant orange-red tulip-like flowers surrounding large brown boat-shaped seed pods. This tree is so radiant when in bloom it is often referred to as "the flame of the forest".

To truly enjoy the wondrous flora of St. Lucia, a relaxed stroll through Mamiku Gardens is highly recommended. *(see Sightseeing Spectacular, page 54)*. To venture into the wilds leads to the discovery of wonders that only Mother Nature could have created.

The mangrove and marsh areas of the island are perhaps the most life-sustaining of all the island's habitats. A multitude of interesting bird species can be found in both areas, while the mangrove also provides a hatching ground for a host of marine life.

The weathered cliffs of the extreme north and Atlantic coasts of St. Lucia harbour **cacti** and the **century plant** and the crevices of the volcanic rock face provides a home to nesting ocean birds such as noddies, terns, and gulls.

At every turn St. Lucia holds a natural wonder – from cool mountain tops to dramatic weather-beaten cliffs. Exploration is a must!

nature

heritage

Who knows how to reveal all of St. Lucia's secret natural assets? Who can bring to the fore all the unique aspects of the island – the aspects that make the St. Lucian experience completely different from any other in the Caribbean? The only answer is, quite naturally, a St. Lucian. This is the philosophy behind Nature Heritage Tourism – an innovative scheme based on creating a unique experience for visitors that is wholly stage-managed by St. Lucians.

The Nature Heritage Tourism project is being developed for many worthwhile reasons, but the most important is because many visitors to St. Lucia do not come for just for the sun, sea and sand. They are motivated by the island's natural environment, its peace and tranquillity and cultural heritage.

Nature Heritage Tourism is a mixture of eco-tourism and adventure tourism. The

stipulations and constraints surrounding eco-tourism alone are far too costly for St. Lucia to consider. In addition, there are already several large resorts on the island that attract the type of mass tourism incompatible with eco-tourism regulations.

The charm about Nature Heritage is that it is available to everyone. It is designed to appeal to visitors who might just want to sample traditional local cuisine, or others who may want to climb Gros Piton, or spend days hiking in search of the island's spectacular waterfalls. Nature Heritage Tourism is all about experiencing all the extraordinary wonders that are St. Lucia.

One of the most important features of the Nature Heritage project revolves around placing tourism development into the hands of the St. Lucian people. Indeed, many of the island's natural assets including waterfalls, hot springs, rainforest acreage, historical sites and even abandoned estate houses belong to private citizens.

The Nature Heritage project is designed to help any St. Lucian who wants to turn their property into a tourist attraction. Assistance is provided in the

form of preparing feasibility studies, providing essential training programmes and even helping to attract financial assistance in order to sustainably transform their properties.

The Nature Heritage concept also aims to increase the room count, which is still well below its optimum capacity. The long-term plan is to construct lodges and log cabins in the rainforest, to restore rundown plantation houses and to encourage St. Lucians to build guest houses which are complimentary to the natural surroundings.

In areas where identified Nature Heritage sites do not belong to private citizens – places such as the Anse La Raye waterfall and Gros Piton – the programme encourages the participation of St. Lucians living in nearby communities. In the case of the Anse La Raye waterfall, for example, the idea is to use local guides and to encourage visitors to stop off in the village, where an interpretation and refreshment centre is planned. Another attraction being developed in Anse La Raye is a Saturday night fish fry. Anse La Raye is a fishing community and the fish fry is an ideal way to bring additional income into the village.

Photographs clockwise from top: the dazzling torch ginger produces a large spike bearing a pink conical head of flowers; dense tropical forests blanket the interior of St. Lucia; sparkling waterfall in the heart of the rainforest; dazzling shades of bougainvillea is a common sight on St. Lucia; abundant tropical flora thrives on St. Lucia; the pretty fishing village of Anse La Raye. Centre: The ancient banyan tree.

Situated at the foot of Gros Piton is the community of Fond Gens Libre, meaning "place of the free people". This small, old settlement dates back to the days of the maroons, when slaves fled the plantations and went to live in the most inaccessible parts of the island. The local people of Fond Gens Libre have always maintained a fierce tradition of independence. However, their community is no longer a secret, as it is situated on the pathway that leads to the summit of the Gros Piton. For the people of Fond Gens Libre, however, this provides a good opportunity for employment. The Nature Heritage programme provides training programmes for people who want to become mountain guides and for those who are willing to set up a first aid and refreshment base in the community.

One of the most ambitious projects of the Nature Heritage programme is the establishment of the National Botanical Gardens. A 90-acre (36-hectare) site on St. Lucia's west coast has already been identified as the ideal place for the gardens. Within this area, an initial inventory has shown that forty plant species and ten exotic birds – including the indigenous St. Lucia oriole – already call the place home. Once the Botanical Gardens are established, more tropical plant and tree species will be introduced. Trails will be developed and ornamental gardens planted. Facilities will be

installed for bird-watching, and the more energetic visitors will be able to hike to the nearby waterfalls. The Botanical Gardens will also include research facilities, a herbarium and nursery.

The Nature Heritage programme envisages that the Botanical Garden will – due to its proximity to Castries and the fact that it will be able to handle a large visitor capacity – attract large numbers of cruise ship visitors thus generating employment for the nearby community. The National Botanical Garden will require tour guides and gardeners, and will rely on the surrounding farming community to provide the necessary produce to supply the restaurant facilities. A second construction phase will include eco-lodges.

The members of St. Lucia's Nature Heritage Tourism office are actively seeking other possible projects to develop. Prior to this initiative, many St. Lucians were unable to raise the necessary funding to cover the investment costs of developing tourism-based projects. Now, they will be be able to participate in the island's tourism industry – an industry that is the island's largest source of foreign exchange.

From every dimension Nature Heritage Tourism is an attractive initiative for St. Lucia. According to the programme's general manager, everyone will benefit from Nature Heritage Tourism. The programme not only provides St. Lucians with new and important avenues for earning an income, but what is more important, it will enhance the tourism industry by offering an authentic St. Lucian experience. It will also diversify the tourism product by opening up many kinds of new market opportunities.

Opposite: The magnificent Gros Piton.
Below: Exotic orchid in the National Botanical Garden.

wild things

O ut of total devastation, the most violent upheaval known to Nature, comes creation. A line of weakness found in the foundation of the earth lies beneath the vastness of the Caribbean Sea. During the early stages of the Tertiary period, this fault line yielded to the immense pressures of the churning, molten mantle, resulting in massive volcanic eruptions, ripping the soul of the earth and giving birth to the Caribbean Volcanic Arc.

St. Lucia is a progeny of these times – an island born by up lifting and grand expulsions of lava rock.

Slowly life began to float ashore; logs and mats of vegetation freed by flooding along the river basin of the Orinoco in South America transported vegetable and animal life, dispersing it along the island chain. Thus the black volcanic mass of St. Lucia gradually became cloaked in botanical species from South America, occasionally interspersed with variants dropped by passing or settling birds. As the island developed into a flourishing habitat, various bird species began to nestle among oceanside crags and thickening forests.

Left: The iguana was introduced to St. Lucia many years ago and are still found in the wild. Opposite: Tiny lizards are found throughout the island.

Lurking lizards

The first inhabitants of the island would have been reptiles and amphibians – hardy animals that were able to survive the tossing and turning of their tiny rafts of log and clumps of herbage. The primitive-looking iguana was once so abundant on St. Lucia that the early Carib settlers dubbed the island *Iouanaloa*, translating to "land of the iguana".

These lizards are extremely adaptable, being aquatic, arboreal, terrestrial and able to survive harsh, desert-like conditions. The iguana, which can grow up to 6 feet (2 metres) in length including its long, whip-like tail, is mostly green, but does have some brown pigmentation. By expanding these particular cells it can achieve a better camouflage. Unfortunately mankind, from the ancient Amerindians to more modern times, has found the iguana to be a tasty part of their diet. Thus, even though the species is currently protected by the St. Lucia Wildlife Act, very few exist in the wild today.

The members of the *anolis* grouping, or *zandoli* in Creole, are distant relations to the iguana. These are the various tree lizards that are common island-wide. Three species exist but they are close kin and difficult to distinguish. In general they range from brilliant green to a duller brownish-green. They are interesting to observe – especially the males, who have intricate fighting and mating rituals which involves the expansion of the throat pouch, hissing, head-bobbing and tail-raising.

At night the mysterious **mabouya** lurks in dark crevices and hidden corners of walls and ceilings. These lizards have unique foot pads that give them the ability to adhere to virtually any surface. Due to their eerie, almost translucent appearance, and the fact that if they happen to accidentally fall on a human, the suction of their feet can be distinctly felt (even to the extent that local legend claims they can suck human blood), they have developed an undeserved evil reputation. The name mabouya is actually that of one of the Carib's most devilish spirits. This harmless lizard is more commonly known as the night lizard and is a member of the gecko family.

The Maria Islands ground lizard, locally known as *zandoli te*, is an endemic species only found on the small islets off the Maria Islands coast of Vieux Fort. This unique creature is under strict protection from the government of St. Lucia. With the help of the Jersey Wildlife Preservation Trust, a new colony has been established on Praslin Island slightly further to the north. It is a magnificent sight with its yellow belly, shiny black throat and brilliant cobalt tail. Trips to the Maria Islands are arranged by the St. Lucia National Trust (*See Sightseeing Spectacular page 50*).

Serpents friendly and fierce

Among the other reptiles washed upon the shores of St. Lucia were at least five known species of snake. The black **cribo** is now extinct, probably due to the later arrival of the mongoose.

venom. Anybody bitten by any snake should seek immediate medical attention, especially if there is any question concerning which species it may be.

St. Lucia also boasts the "world's smallest snake". The 6-inch (15-cm) **leptotyphlops** lives underground and is very rarely seen. It is brown with two stripes running along its back. It is practically blind due to the fact that in lives in the soil.

The **couresse** is a harmless little grass snake that has been declared the "world's rarest snake". Like the *zandoli te*, it is found only on the tiny Maria Islands.

The **boa constrictor** is the most commonly found and the largest of the island's snakes. Although they are generally light brown with darker crossbars, when viewed in the sunlight they become almost iridescenct. They are easily distinguished from the one viper found on the island by its squared-off snout. Its chunky head accounts for the local name *tete chien* or dog's

The **fer de lance**, however, is a "serpent of a different colour". This pit viper is unpredictable and pugnacious. The colour varies from grey to brownish-grey with a pattern similar to the diamond-backed rattler. The head is shaped in the traditional serpent arrowhead allowing for its poison glands. The *fer de lance* is

This 3-foot (1-metre) reptile is olive-brown with a black pattern. It is believed to have once inhabited the main island, but was forced onto the islets as man's activities increased.

head. They feed on small animals and secure their prey by wrapping around the victim's body and constricting the intake of air to the lungs. They are not large enough, and definitely not aggressive enough, to constrict humans.

only found in an isolated band stretching east to west across the island from Dennery to Anse La Raye. They tend to avoid areas of frequent activity. Their bite is extremely poisonous, but the hospitals are equipped with anti-

One of the sweetest night sounds of St. Lucia comes surprisingly from the male **tree frog** as he calls his mate. Here in nature, the dream of many men has come true – the female has no voice!

Feathered fauna

As the flora of St. Lucia developed and small reptiles and amphibians began to prosper, birds discovered a new home. Many South American species hopped the island chain. This resulted in many of the Caribbean islands having birds of the same family. However, due to their isolation on different islands over many years, some unique species subsequently evolved.

A prime example is the **St. Lucian parrot**. Of the same Amazona family which is found throughout the islands, the *Amazona versicolor* is unique to St. Lucia. Predominantly green, it has a violet head, orange chest, and brilliant yellow feathers under its wings, which are tipped in indigo blue. It demonstrates a variety of calls, but is generally heard "squawking" as it flies overhead.

Only a few years ago, it was considered extremely endangered, but thanks to the combined efforts of the Jersey Zoo and the St. Lucian Forestry Department, the fate of this splendid bird has been saved. There are now thought to be over 500 living in the wild in the rainforest.

Also endemic is the **St. Lucian oriole**. This beautiful, medium-sized bird is mostly black, with a vibrant orange on its wings and rump. This shy bird is generally found in deeply-forested areas, but is not restricted to the rainforest. Its song is a series of melodious whistles. It is distantly related to the common, gregarious **Carib grackle**, a glossy black bird with a shrill squeak of a whistle. This bird is frequently seen around the hotels, especially at meal times.

A few of St. Lucia's native species are becoming extremely rare. The **Semper's warbler**, a small grey bird with pale, nearly white feet is also shy – so much so that its song has never been clearly identified.

The **forest thrush**, although found on a few neighbouring islands, is very rare in St. Lucia. This deep brown bird is easily identified by its bright orange feet, bill and orbital ring. The **white-breasted thrasher**, another unsociable bird, survives only in the northern section of St. Lucia and one area of Martinique. It is mostly sooty brown, but has a dazzling white breast.

Opposite: The timid agouti. Centre: The Maria Islands ground lizard. Below: Boa constrictor in the small zoo at Union.

Other forest birds of particular interest include the light blue-grey **Adelaide's warbler**, with its yellow and white markings. Close in size and appearance is the **banana quit**.

The island boasts three types of **hummingbird**: the tiny **Antillean crested**, with its bright emerald crest; the **purple-throated Carib**, a very dark-coloured bird with a vivid burgundy throat (they also have some green on their wings and a long, thin beak); and the **green-throated Carib**, which has a vibrant blue-green throat patch.

In addition to the many forest and garden birds, St. Lucia's coastline and wetlands play host to numerous colourful sea and marsh birds.

The gawky **moorhen** is black with a scarlet frontal shield. It resembles a cross between a chicken and a duck as it paddles nervously along the river's edge, among the reeds. The velvety-**little blue heron**, the **great blue heron**, the **green-backed heron** and the **yellow-crested night heron** often grace the marshes, rivers and mangrove areas.

Below: Tree lizards are common throughout the island and vary in colour from brilliant green to a dull brown.

The coastal cliffs and marshy inlets provide the perfect environment for several species of terns and tropics including the **brown noddy**, the **laughing gull**, the **brown booby** and the magnificent **frigate bird**, with its vast wingspan of up to 6 feet (2 metres).

The birds of the island have generally found a natural path of migration which began thousands of years ago with the original immigrants from South America. The **cattle egret** is thought to have crossed the Atlantic from Africa in more recent years. This white bird is capped with a small patch of bright yellow which is especially noticeable in mating plumage. It is most easily recognized, though, by the fact that it normally feeds among grazing livestock, which churn up an instant insect smorgasbord as they walk along.

It is not just the tourist who find refuge from blustery winters in St. Lucia's warm tropical climate: feathered migrants include the **kestrel, osprey, kingfisher,** and **purple martin**.

Other Creatures

Mammals were introduced to St. Lucia by the Arawak Indians, who transported their own food supplies as they travelled northward from South America. Apart from fruit and vegetables, they carried tiny animals which would be nurtured, but not totally domesticated. The **opossum** was one and the other, perhaps less commonly known, was the **agouti**. This timid creature is best described as looking like a cross between a guinea pig and a rabbit. They are vegetarian and grow to the size of smaller rabbit breeds. There are only a few left in quiet areas of the island, but they can be seen at the mini-zoo at Union.

The **mongoose** was "the sure cure for the *fer de lance*" – or so it was thought. However, this creature decided that the eggs of the black cribo and several ground-nesting birds made for a more convenient meal – thus the extinction of a few endemic species.

St. Lucia is home to a dazzling array of nature's delights and visitors should take the time to explore the "wild side" of this enchanted paradise.

natural habitats

A tiny dot in Caribbean Sea, the island of St. Lucia is just under 248 square miles (640 sq km). The towering landscape of the mountainous centre draws in the rain clouds that feed the dense rainforest thus providing a safe habitat for a multitude of animal and bird species. Providing a stark contrast are the barren, dry, volcanic cliffs of the Atlantic coastline, which are battered by constant wind and salt. In yet another example of Mother Nature's marvel, plants have adapted to these bleak conditions – and thrive!

The island's rivers begin high in the mountains with tiny trickles becoming surging cascades that spread across verdant banana plantations before they flow into the Carribean Sea. In the areas, where salty habitats meet fresh water rivers, brackish conditions give rise to the tangling roots of the mangrove.

There is an incredible diversity in the natural habitats of St. Lucia, all of which await discovery and and exploration.

Rainforest

When entering the rainforest on any of the several hikes offered by the Forestry Division (see *Bird Watching Trips and Forest Walks* , *page 101)*, visitors will notice the trees gradually become larger, both in height and girth. The further one progresses into the depths of the forest, the grander these arboreal sentinels become.

The **gommier** is an indigenous species of the *bruseraceae* family. This evergreen sprouts up to 120 feet (36 metres) and its bulging base helps to support its massive height. Its canopy consists of ovate leaves that dip at the end to act as a water spout, letting the rain drip easily to the ground below. Its clusters of flowers are tiny and a delicate green in colour but tend to go unnoticed as they are obscured by the vastness of the tree. This tree played an vital role in the island's heritage as it was used by the Amerindians to fashion their canoes.

The **chataigner** is an elegant tree, with large expanding buttresses at the base which help to support its towering mass. These buttresses can dwarf humans – often growing to over 12 feet (4 metres).

Another marvel of the rainforests is the **awali.** Starting out as a minute plant seated on the limb of a larger tree, the awali sends out tendril roots hanging like vines from their high perch. Gradually the tendrils find earth and take hold, thickening into substantial roots. Slowly the awali prospers – at the expense of its original host which is strangled by the many dangling roots. The red berries of the awali form an important part of the diet for the St. Lucian parrot. Man, too, benefits as the roots are woven into wicker baskets.

The forest floor is thick with several varieties of fern. The most outstanding is the **tree fern**, a medium-sized tree which is topped with a giant parasol of spreading, lacy ferns. This species is one of the world's oldest and has changed little since prehistoric times.

Birds finding refuge in the depths of the rainforest include the St. Lucian parrot, the St. Lucian oriole, the Antillean peewee, the black finch and several species of thrush and thrasher.

Coastal regions

Due to the constant trade winds and the salty conditions, the rocky outcrops edging the Atlantic coast provide a harsh environment. The winds whisk any threatening rain to drench the higher mountain tops, leaving the black coastal rocks barren and inhospitable.

Evolution and adaptation have provided a minimal habitat and

Mangrove

In the estuaries where the rivers meet the sea, a unique habitat exists. The water is neither fresh nor salt, but a brackish mixture. Here, plants have adapted to provide this salty environment with vegetation. The long roots of the red mangrove reach deep into the water to take hold in the river bed. Small breathing pores cover the prop roots to take advantage of all available air. The filtration system of the props allows water, but not salt, to be absorbed. Even the seeds have adapted. They grow as long spikes on the tree before falling spear-like into the depths, submerging into the soil.

The wetlands are rimmed with the tall, black mangrove. As its dangling roots drop into the water, an extension grows back upward into the air. The plant actually ingests the salt which it then emits back through the leaves.

The white mangrove grows further from the water's edge than the red and black varieties. It has breathing glands, and the ability to drop prop roots if necessary. These trees usually grow side by side with the button tree – so named because of its button-like seeds.

several species have evolved sufficiently to flourish under these adverse conditions. The cactus is a good example.

The **prickly pear** consists of flat, fleshy segments stacked in an incongruent pattern. It radiates thin spiky needles which absorb moisture from the air. The fleshy pulp stores water and thus this plant has security.

The St. Lucia coastline is visited by various gulls, terns and tropicbirds. Cattle egrets roost among the cliffs and frigatebirds, searching for ultimate sanctuary have found a haven in the remote Fregate Island.

Background: Towering ferns in the rainforest. Above: Magnificent stands of bamboo are found deep in the rainforest. Opposite: The St. Lucia parrot.

Another wetlands plant is the **seaside mahoe**. It is a small member of the hibiscus or *malvaceae* family. The flowers are pale yellow and resemble a partially-open hibiscus blossom. The unripe seeds produce a yellow dye.

The mangrove swamps shelter an abundance of life. The long roots of the red mangrove trap leaf litter and earth debris as it flows into the sea; therefore the waters and soil are bursting with nutrients. Some ocean fish and crustaceans actually seek out the safety of the mangrove root system to lay their eggs. The fish subsequently hatch to find an excellent food supply.

Bird life also thrives here with many wetland birds frequenting the inlets to feast on the bountiful fish and insect population. St. Lucia's wetland birds include several types of heron, as well as the great and snowy egret. The belted kingfisher, a blue-grey bird with a white band across its chest, is also frequently seen fishing the lagoons and mangrove swamps.

Shrub lands

Although the vegetation may appear less spectacular than the rainforest, the shrub lands and drier forests contain some fascinating trees and the largest selection of bird life on the island.

The **bois d'Inde** is a small tree with smooth grey bark. The shiny green leaves are elliptic and have a similar smell to allspice. A less common variety has leaves that smell of lemon. The leaves of both are sometimes brewed up as a pleasant-tasting tea to relieve colds.

The **campeche** or **logwood** is a valuable tree. The extremely hard wood is often used to fashion the pillars that support homes in the countryside. It is slow burning and long lasting when made into charcoal. The French propagated vast logwood groves in order to produce a red dye. Its flowers give off a heady perfume which is a favourite of the honey bee. Beware as the limbs have sharp thorns.

The dwarf **gommier** is cousin to the grand species found in the rainforest, but only grows to medium height here. The resin of the tree has properties similar to turpentine and it is locally referred to as the "turpentine tree". The Carib Indians used the sap to treat internal bruises and sprains. Its shiny red bark is most unusual as it is constantly peeling. St. Lucians refer to it as the "tourist tree", because of its likeness to careless visitors – red and peeling from sunburn!

The lower forests teem with a mixture of forest and shrub birds, including the St. Lucian oriole, the black finch and bullfinch, the yellow warbler, Adelaide's warbler, the nocturnal St. Lucian nightjar, the pewee, the mangrove cuckoo, and the blue-hooded euphonia.

Bird-Watching and Forest Hikes

A variety of nature-oriented trips can be arranged by the Department of Forestry (Tel. 450-2078). Trips to the rainforest are only permitted when accompanied by a forestry guide, both to guarantee your safety and to protect the natural habitats of the island's wildlife.

HIKES IN THE RAINFOREST

Barre de l'Isle

This trail is located along the mountain range that separates the northern section of the island from the south. It is about a twenty-minute drive from Castries just past L'Abbaye on a right turning off the highway. The walk up to the foot of **Morne La Combe** takes approximately one hour and provides some good sightings of the chataigner, the tree fern, the Caribbean heliconia and other plant life. The St. Lucian parrot is occasionally seen in this area. A further hour of more rigorous trekking takes visitors to the breathtaking crest of the Morne to reveal a vista of unsurpassed and incredible beauty.

Des Cartiers

This trail requires a medium level of fitness. A three-hour loop takes visitors into the heart of the rainforest from the Mahaut side. The start is slightly inland, just north of Micoud – about a one hour drive from Castries.

A huge variety of botanical life exists here and there is a good chance of at least hearing the St. Lucian parrot as it flies overhead.

A longer hike takes visitors on a four- to five-hour loop through the interior across to the other side of the forest.

Enbas Saut Falls Trail

This is a picturesque three-hour trail which is accessible from Soufrière. It is incredibly scenic with a combination of rainforest, cloud forest, elfin woodland and unique wildlife. The trail leads to a sparkling waterfall and bathing in its cascading waters is a great experience. The trail requires a good level of fitness.

Forestière Trail

This hike begins at Piton Flora, along the mountain range which rises behind Castries. The drive to the trail takes about forty-five minutes. Several species of birds can be seen along this walk, which is not quite as strenuous as some of the others. The trail, shaded by towering trees, meanders through a section of ancient rainforest.

Background: The magnificent rainforest in St. Lucia. Above: Delicate ferns abound in the rainforest area. Centre: The wax rose. Right: Green sea turtles nest on the eastern shores of St. Lucia.

BIRD-WATCHING TOURS

Bird-watching tours are available through the Forestry Department and can be customized to suit particular requirements. Enthusiasts can select from trips to the Bois d'Orange Wetland, the Mankote Mangrove, a forest trail at Desbarras or a trail through the rainforest. The knowledgeable guides have studied the local birdlife extensively.

Turtle-watching

It is not only birds that visit remote cliffs and offshore islets to find peaceful nesting spots – turtles also seek haven on the eastern shores of St. Lucia to lay their eggs in safety. During nightfall, between the months of March to August, the cumbersome leatherback turtle

slowly lumbers ashore to lay its eggs. Before daybreak, the turtles retun to the sea, leaving their eggs blanketed in the warmth of the sand. Two months later, the baby turtles hatch and instinctively scramble towards the sea.

Leatherback turtles are unique because their shells are made of distinct bone ridges covered with a black, leathery carapace. The Atlantic green turtle and the hawksbill turtle also visit St. Lucia to lay their eggs.

A "turtle-watch group" operates during the nesting months. To join one of these unique excursions contact Jim Sparks at 452-9829. Be prepared to walk the beach all night and bring your own torch, snacks, water and warm clothing.

a place

All the different peoples who have lived on St. Lucia have had their own distinct building methods. But despite all their imaginative architectural concepts, the designs have been tempered by the island's climate, topography and availability of building materials.

The Amerindians, who had no knowledge of how to work iron, built environmentally-friendly, communal homes called *carbets*. These wattle structures were made from plaited branches and covered with thatched roofs of tightly-bound grasses. They were easy to maintain and repair. The breeze circulated through the latticework walls and brought welcome currents of cool air to the *carbet's* interior.

Hurricanes were a constant cause of concern, and whenever these violent storms struck, they invariably devastated lighter structures. However, due to their simple design, they could quickly be rebuilt once the bad weather had passed.

Photographs: St. Lucian houses are traditionally built from wood and include features such as delicate filigree fretwork, jalousie shutters, wooden balconies and overhanging roofs. The buildings are often painted in bright colours or incorporate interesting murals in their design.

Europeans came with images imprinted on their homesick minds of the places they had left behind. However, the St. Lucian terrain forced these settlers to rethink the building traditions of the mother country. Instead of constructing homes that kept the cold out, St. Lucia's heat and humidity – not to mention the hordes of disease-bearing mosquitoes found in the lower elevations (yellow fever and malaria used to be major causes of death) – forced the settlers to seek out the cooler hilltops to construct open-plan homes that permitted the free circulation of air. Indeed, keeping cool was a major preoccupation when it came to building a home in St. Lucia.

The plantation houses were traditionally built from wood and positioned in such a way to afford a good view over as much of the estate as possible. Large balconies surrounded the house. Overhanging roofs allowed the light to come in, but blocked out the direct sun. Fretwork was attached to the eaves around the house and carved with delicate filigree motifs. The extended balconies prevented the direct sunlight from reaching the main walls of the house and, even at the hottest time of the day, the

to live

temperature inside was usually pleasantly cool.

Wooden jalousie windows let in the maximum amount of breeze and could be tilted slightly to keep out prying eyes. But the occupants of the house could look out and watch unseen everything taking place outside the house.

An additional set of exterior shutters were added to protect the house in times of bad weather. Roof angles were also carefully calculated to resist extreme weather conditions. (It was discovered that flat roofs caved in during hurricanes).

However, it took years of trial and error for certain colonial contractors to appreciate the power of nature. One of the earlier versions of **Government House** was so unsuitable to the local climate that it collapsed in a hurricane, killing the Governor. It was rebuilt in 1893 by British engineers, incorporating some of the essential features to prevent the future occurence of any similar disaster.

Plantation houses such as **Balembouche** in Choiseul and **Errand** at Dennery are excellent examples of traditional estate houses. Two hundred years ago,

plantations were around Castries with cultivated fields extending all along the town's boundaries.

In the towns, the structures were predominantly built from timber. Homeowners were obliged to find ingenious ways of keeping the interiors cool. Important towns such as Castries and Soufrière were phenomenally hot, as they were situated in a natural valley surrounded by high hills.

Large rosette cut-outs were set into attics and into exterior walls on the upper floors. This helped take advantage of what little wind circulated. An ingenious cooling system was created by placing large blocks of ice on window ledges. Water from the melting blocks ran off the roof, while the breeze blew ice-cooled draughts into the house.

Over the years much of St. Lucia's architectural heritage has sadly taken a severe battering. Natural

disasters, such as a devastating hurricane in the late 1700s, flattened many of the island's historical buildings.

The French Revolution also took its toll on St. Lucian architecture. Revolutionary forces and bands of runaway slaves who formed themselves into guerrilla armies set out to destroy everything that reminded them of slavery's oppression.

Prosperous plantation towns – such as Dauphin on the north-Atlantic coast – no longer exist, a victim of the Revolution's violence. The plantation house at **Mamiku Estate** near Praslin was destroyed in one of the most casualty-ridden battles between the British and Maroon forces.

Over the years much of St. Lucia's urban architecture has been consumed by fire. Between 1796 and 1948, Castries was destroyed by four fires. Half of Soufrière, St. Lucia's first capital, was also razed to the ground.

The buildings that have withstood the island's fire and hurricanes are the impressive Catholic churches. These massive structures appear to dominate most of the major towns and villages. In Soufrière, the Catholic church is visible from most points in the town. The building's huge roof was once the town's most efficient water catchment, and the inhabitants relied heavily upon it.

The Europeans specialised in military fortifications and St. Lucia was one of the most fought-over

Photographs: Traditional homes in Soufrière and Castries.

Caribbean islands. At Vigie peninsula, the entire headland is covered with artillery emplacements and military barracks. Vigie, which means "lookout point" in French, was the northern defence line for Castries Harbour. At the southern entrance of this greatly-prized port, Morne Fortune and Tapion Point were also heavily defended by cannon. The soldiers' barracks and administrative buildings demonstrate the huge military presence and strategic importance of these sites.

Another highly-prized military base is found at **Pigeon Island National Park**. Now attached to the mainland, this once small islet used to be an almost self-sufficient military outpost. The British used it to spy on French activities in nearby Martinique. The earliest buildings date back to the 1700s and are built predominantly of stone. The presence of a lime kiln on Pigeon Island along with recently discovered evidence of tuff – a versatile, volcanic rock – could indicate one of the earliest uses of concrete in the world.

In addition to the stone structures, many of the military buildings throughout St. Lucia are built from thousands of clay bricks brought in boats from France and England as ballast. Once off-loaded, they were transformed into some of the most solid structures that still stand today in St. Lucia. The thick walls not only withstood enemy attack, but were perfect temperature regulators, keeping out the heat and maintaining a cool interior.

compounds are still based on African models. In many rural areas, the design of many homes are typically African. They consist of three structures set in a circular or triangular pattern. The main house, for sleeping and socialising, is usually a simple timber structure elevated on stone or concrete piles. These posts encourage the circulation of air beneath the house and prevent insects and unwanted pests from getting into the house.

Situated away from the main building is a simple structure that serves as a kitchen. The second outhouse is a pit toilet, known in Creole as a *pwivet*.

surrounded with an enclosure to ensure privacy.

Today, St. Lucian architecture borrows from numerous influences. Timber has largely been replaced with an easy-to-maintain, solid cement, but in and around communities like Laborie, Choiseul and Soufrière, there is still a wealth of well-preserved, traditional wooden houses. Indeed, Soufrière is in the process of restoring many of the wooden houses spared by the fire.

Many old plantation houses are open to the public and Pigeon Island National Park, with its historical fortifications, is a must-see for visitors. *(See Sightseeing Spectacular, pages 30/31).*

One of the earliest and most innovative military structures was built in Soufrière in 1785 by decree of King Louis XIV. The **Diamond Mineral Baths** were originally constructed for the sole purpose of rejuvenating battle-weary French soldiers. The therapeutic benefits of Soufrière's sulphurous waters compared favourably with the waters of Aix-les-Bains in France.

The island's African heritage has also influenced its architectural traditions. Village and community

The main houses were also built in such a way that they could be easily dismantled in sections and transported to another site. Much of the St. Lucian peasantry leased their land, and when the time came to move on, people literally packed up their houses and rebuilt them at a new location. It was easy to rebuild kitchens, and new latrines simply had to be dug and

culture

Many of St. Lucia's cultural traditions, especially the island's dances and songs, have only recently been documented. Slaves did not record their ancient ceremonies for fear of reprisal and their customs thus became a form of underground art that represented a secret solidarity among the oppressed societies.

According to Harold Simmons, one of the first St. Lucians to document local tradition, this solidarity was always at variance with established authority, orthodox religion, upper class morality and the law.

Fortunately, today's social mechanisms no longer suppress traditional expression. Indeed, with the establishment of the Folk Research Centre – with its mandate to resuscitate and record St. Lucian culture – all the Creole songs, dances and ceremonies are being encouraged and are making a comeback.

In St. Lucia there are three special traditions that are found nowhere else in the Caribbean.

Left: In this painting of The Black Madonna *by Dunstan St. Omer, the traditional Biblical images have been replaced by those of local people and black is used as a primary colour in a complete reversal of the psychology of white being good and black being evil.*

Kélé

Kélé is a ceremony of ancestral worship that is only practiced in the north-eastern community of Babonneau. Kélé was introduced in 1867, twenty years after Emancipation, with the arrival of members of the Ekiti tribe from western Nigeria. Community members who wish to pay homage to a dead ancestor contact the Kélé priest in Babonneau who organises a day-long ceremony that also involves the sacrifice of a ram. The songs that accompany the Kélé service are all of African origin and most of the rites are performed to the rhythm of the tambour (drum).

Floral societies

There are two floral societies in St. Lucia – La Rose and La Marguerite. The origins of these societies have been lost, but anthropologists believe they were created by slaves in search of their own social identity.

Each society has its own kings, queens, dukes, generals, matrons, magistrates, nurses, soldiers and police. Next to the king, the most important personality is the chantwelle, (lead singer), who sets the rhythm for the society's gatherings at which traditional songs, dances and ceremonies are performed.

The traditional colours of La Rose are red, pink and white. The society is named after St. Rose de Lima, the first Christian saint of the New World, and their feast day is 30 August. The colours of La Marguerite are blue and white, and the society's patron saint is St. Marguerite Mary Alacoque of France. Their feast day is 17 October. (See Festivals, page 120).

On feast days, which begin with a mass and are followed with a procession, special performances are held at the Cultural Centre in Castries. Efforts are being made to revive both the La Rose and La Marguerite festivals.

The La Rose society has a much broader appeal and considers members of La Marguerite snobbish, while La Marguerites think that La Rose members are inferior. Rivalry between the two societies used to erupt into violent public confrontations, but these days enmity is expressed only in taunting songs.

Folk songs and stories

Many of St. Lucia's old folk songs are a fusion of African and European cultures. The Quadrille, the Polka, la Cormette and la Grande Ronde are dances of European origin.

Local folk musicians have, however, given these European numbers a distinct African flavour. The folk orchestras in St. Lucia are led by violin masters such as the great Rameau Poleon. Banjos, guitars and percussion instruments called chak chaks are all vital to local folk ensembles. At special events, a chantwelle joins the musicians. The greatest St. Lucian chantwelle is a woman called Sessenne.

Many traditional songs have been composed to accompany various social gestures of solidarity. Songs are sung for coup de main (helping hand), when an entire community gets together to help one of its members build a house or clear a piece of land. There are special drinking sonnets for A Bwe or drinking parties. For beach parties or full moon get-togethers, there is another set of appropriate compositions.

When it comes to outdoor parties, traditional story telling is often part of the evening's activities. A konte or storyteller starts every tale with the word "kwik." The audience has to reply

"e *dit kwak*" to indicate that they are listening. At key moments during his rendition, the *konte* will call out "*kwik*", and an immediate response is expected from the audience to indicate that everyone is still awake.

The practice of story telling has permitted *Anancy Spider*, *Compère Lapin* (both similar to *Brer Rabbit* stories) and countless other folk tales to be passed down through the generations. The *konte* tradition is also at the heart of St. Lucia's popular theatre.

Like many of the folk stories, the popular theatre performances nearly always have a moral

Above: The St. Lucia Jazz Festival is a popular annual event. Opposite: The origin of the coalpot remains a mystery. The teso, as it is known in Creole, is found nowhere else in the Caribbean.

lesson for the audience. Many of today's themes teach youngsters to respect their elders and emphasize the importance of protecting and preserving the environment.

St. Lucia's most popular stage actor is George Alphonse. "Fish", as he is known in St. Lucia and throughout the Caribbean, was originally destined for priesthood, but the seminary did not suit his theatrical temperament and his devotion is now to theatre and comedy. He has created several characters – including "Country Boy" and "Grandpa", through which he tells his stories. Despite his serious messages, Fish is extremely amusing.

Musical messages

On a regional scale, the calypso message that originated in Trinidad and Tobago is now firmly implanted in St. Lucia. This integral part of the island's culture was (and still is) an interesting means of sharing a wide range of perspectives on topical issues.

Social commentary, satire and emotion are the name of the calypso game. Calypsonians like Pep, Educator, Invader and Ashanti entertain audiences each year with racy lyrics and hot musical beats. "Lord Help Me", one of the most skilful social commentators, has sung about everything from the high price of local produce to the inability of islanders to mind their own business. Herb Black, a Rastafarian calypsonian has a repertoire that ranges from songs about Nelson Mandela to the fact that life is so hard in St. Lucia that "one day's work won't buy me a pair of shoes".

Singing calypso is a serious business, and even a previous Minister of Culture was a calypsonian. The Honourable Damian Greaves was better known onstage as "Short Pants".

The St. Lucian love affair with calypso is particularly strong during carnival. However, there are some musicians who are so versatile that their melodies are appropriate all year round.

Luther François is probably the finest musician to emerge from this island. And, while he plays virtually every instrument, he prefers the saxophone. He composes, arranges and plays with such dexterity and soul that he has earned the respect of the biggest names in the business.

Boo Hinkson became a professional musician at the age of fourteen. When he was still in his teens he headed one of the most popular bands to emerge from the Caribbean. In their heyday, the Tru Tones played dance music, jazz, ballads, old songs, and original numbers. They travelled extensively and were once the special guests at the Super Bowl.

The band is no longer together but Boo Hinkson remains in the music business as a composer and solo guitarist.

Jazz, too, has its place on the island. The introduction of the St. Lucia Jazz Festival in 1992 led to the formation of good local jazz ensembles, such as Third Eye.

St. Lucians, especially those in rural areas, also have a curious affection for country and western music. This dates back to World War II when the U.S. established two military bases on the island – one near Gros Islet in the north and a second close to Vieux Fort in the extreme south.

The American servicemen left behind this unusual musical legacy and instead of reggae and calypso, rural discotheques blast Conway Twitty and Jim Reeves. Every year, Radio St. Lucia hosts a country and western dancing competition that draws enthusiastic participants from around the island.

Reggae, ragga and rock music also have their niche in St. Lucia. From Bob Marley to Buju Banton and Michael Jackson, the island is a melting pot of rhythm. St. Lucians love to dance and sing and are frequently seen standing in queues humming a tune or tapping their feet to some invisible melody.

ISLAND ARTISANS

"From creation come the potters – that is how long the potting tradition has existed in St. Lucia". This is the opinion of Mrs. Cathy Osman, a potter from Morne Gouge, a community in Choiseul that nestles in the shadow of Gros Piton.

As in Amerindian times, potting is a woman's domain. The men are only involved when they initially dig the clay out of the earth and deposit it into a suitable hole where it must soak in water for a week before being pounded to an appropriate level of pliability.

The women then take over and create different forms with the raw material. Pots for coal, cooking, flowers and tea, as well as water jugs, are fashioned by hand without the use of a mould. Once the basic shape has been formed, the potter then refines the surfaces by sanding them down with a specially selected sea-stone. They must then dry before being fired.

Cathy Osman specialises in coalpots, cookware and flower pots – heavy items that belie the strength of this slim woman who took over the family tradition of potting some thirty years ago.

Another artisan of clay, Delia Peter, better known as "Auntie", has been a potter for forty years. She prefers to create water carafes, lanterns and tea pots.

Most of the potters' creations are based on ancient designs. However, due to a lack of documentation, countless skills have been lost forever – the Amerindians had developed sophisticated glazing techniques which nobody has been able to reproduce since.

Above: Colourful toy crafts are hand-carved and painted in the village of Choiseul. Centre: Exquisite sculpture by Victor Eudovic. Opposite: Wood carving studio at the Livity Art Studio.

The origin of the coalpot – a simple clay stove still widely used in St. Lucia – remains a mystery. The *teso*, as it is known in Creole, is found nowhere else in the Caribbean.

Prior to the widespread introduction of aluminium and stainless steel pans, St. Lucians cooked their food exclusively in *canaris*, large clay casseroles, made by people like Cathy Osman.

Much of the work produced by local potters is today considered as functional art. The attractive, yet practical pieces are reminders of the years when the island was self-sufficient and had no use for imported items from Europe and the U.S. St. Lucians used to make all their stoves and cookware, as well as their their furniture and basketware. Different techniques were applied to create items as wide-ranging as fish traps (made from plaited bamboo) to wicker chairs made from the fibres of the awali tree.

Indeed, nature provided all the necessary raw materials. *Kus kus* grass, wicker, screw pine and white cedar were all cleverly transformed into utilitarian items that became an integral part of every St. Lucian household.

Despite the fact that potting and other handicraft skills are dying out, there is still a market for much of crafts produced. Cathy Osman makes 200 coalpots a month and finds she has a ready market for every one of them.

The pottery and basket-weaving traditions are particularly strong in Choiseul, a village in the south-west of St. Lucia. Not far from Cathy Osman's home at Morne Gouge is La Pointe Caraîbe, the last stronghold for St. Lucia's Amerindian population.

Many local potters live here, as do basket weavers, makers of fish traps and boat builders. The Amerindians were expert seamen, and canoes are still made according to a thousand-year-old method. Each one is hewn from the single trunk of a giant gommier tree. The canoes are then shaped by fire and water, as well as by hand.

While traditional canoes are found in fishing communities all over the island, locally-made pottery and basketware are readily available at the Castries market and at craft shops around the island such as the Livity Art Studio in Choiseul.

Wonders of wood

Livity is also one of the places to find the wood sculpting of Lawrence Deligny – who is better known to his friends and colleagues as "Uptight".

Uptight, a self-taught sculptor, has been carving unique pieces for the last twenty-five years. He inherited an appreciation for woodwork from his father who was a joiner. However, Uptight realised from a young age that his talent was more for decorative pieces than the fabrication of functional items.

His favourite woods are red and white cedar. Through his art, he tries to portray the traditional lifestyle of St. Lucia and carves elaborate masks and some fabulous fish. The Adam and Eve theme dominates much of his work. He portrays creation's first couple as farmers cultivating the first Caribbean garden. According to Uptight, every piece of wood is trying to say something different and it is his job to bring out each individual story.

He has also carved hundreds of timber supports for hotels around the island, such as Anse Chastanet and Ladera. He also made the giant chess set at the Jalousie Hilton.

The man who has been wood carving in St. Lucia for the longest time is Eudovic. At his studio on the Morne, Victor Eudovic transforms wood into smooth, abstract forms. He uses the direction of the wood grain to produce pieces that virtually reach out to be touched. There is nothing utilitarian about his work – he is quite simply a magnificent artist. He studied his art in Trinidad for ten years before returning to St. Lucia to teach. He later travelled to Nigeria on a UN

scholarship where he studied the traditional art of *Yoruba*, the artistic symbols of the people and their ancient techniques of elaborate sculpture. He returned to St. Lucia after a period of seven months to continue teaching, although he later stopped in order to concentrate on producing unique sculptures for exhibitions. Today, he holds approximately three per year.

He prefers to work with Laurier Canelle, a tree which is now extinct, but Eudovic uses ancient stumps and roots found deep within the rainforest. He also carves in mahogany, teak, and red or white cedar.

Canvas creations

St. Lucian painters are extremely blessed. The landscape and the flora provide the most vibrant palette of colours and textures that only serve to inspire the island's artists.

Llewellyn Xavier is St. Lucia's most internationally acclaimed artist. His work is in the permanent collections of such prestigious galleries as the Metropolitan Museum of Modern Art in New York.

Above: Colourful masks by Zaka make a great souvenir. Below: Murals by Dunstan St. Omer decorate the village walls in Anse La Raye. Centre: Chris Gadjadhar at Zaka carves a unique mask from driftwood. Opposite: Llewellyn Xavier displays one of his canvas masterpieces.

Dunstan St. Omer, on the other hand, has not made such an international name for himself. However, locally and throughout the Caribbean he is known as a talented landscape artist and religious painter. One of his most popular themes is the Madonna and he has produced several

beautiful versions of the Virgin Mary with child. His work adorns the walls of the Cathedral of the Immaculate Conception in Castries, where he painted the colourful murals, as well as the striking altarpiece. In all the altarpieces St. Omer has created for churches around St. Lucia, he portrays Jesus Christ as a black man. "If Christ cannot be black, then what use is he to us," says the artist. In collaboration with his sons, who have all inherited their father's passion and talent, St. Omer has painted outdoor murals on Manoel Street in Castries and in the village of Anse La Raye.

Originally from Dominica, Arnold Toulon has established his art

studio in St. Lucia. He specialises in large, colourful abstracts that take their inspiration from his surroundings. His vibrant work can be seen at the Windjammer Landing Resort.

The work of St. Lucian-born artist Winston Branch is found in many international collections. He paints moody, acrylic abstracts – often on wood and cloth.

Aundrieux John is a young local talent whose work is sold through the St. Lucia Fine Art Gallery. John specialises in computer-generated images and bold graphics that fuse African themes with a host of West Indian personalities.

The talented and beautiful Michelle Elliott, whose work is exhibited at the Coal Pot Restaurant in Vigie Marina, uses bright, colourful pastels to portray her unique interpretation of St. Lucian life. Marine scenes, local architecture and day-to-day life are portrayed in a style that imbued with Michelle's own passion and energy for life.

Another popular artist, Rastafarian Soupçyon, creates reflections of St. Lucian life on silk cloth.

A different type of art can be seen at Zaka Masks and Totems, where wood sculpting is combined with bright Caribbean colours. Chris Gadjadhar and Sophie Barnard, Zaka's owners, carve imaginative masks from driftwood and old timber, exploiting the natural tendency of the wood and revealing faces with hundreds of different expressions. Each mask has its own unique face and painting brings out its personality.

The work of all local artists can be viewed at many galleries around the island.

LLEWELLYN XAVIER

Llewellyn Xavier was born in Choiseul in 1945. He originally planned to become an agriculturist, but after only a few months apprenticeship with the government's agricultural department, Xavier concluded that the farming life was definitely not for him.

In 1961, he moved to Barbados, and it was here he picked up a paintbrush for the first time. To his surprise, his first pieces, (today he calls them "airport art") are all completely sold out. It was this early success that deepened his commitment to become a serious artist.

In 1971, moved by the plight of the Afro-American prisoner, George Jackson, Xavier created a new artistic concept he called "mail art". In order to draw attention to theunjust sentence on Jackson, Xavier mailed him a lithographic work wrapped around the outside of a cardboard tube. Xavier asked Jackson to write his comments and to sign the work.

The tube then acquired visas and stamps and Xavier eventually mailed different works in the Jackson series to John Lennon, Yoko Ono, Jean Genet and James Baldwin for their comments.

A subsequent exhibition of this unique form of art was sponsored by international publishers, Penguin Books and Jonathan Cape, and established Xavier on an international level.

At the age of thirty-four, Xavier enrolled in at the School of the Museum of Fine Art in Boston, Massachusetts. At the same time, he was experiencing strong, religious callings and spent much time in monasteries searching for a truth that eluded him.

In 1987, he married Christina and returned to St. Lucia where he embarked on a contemporary "mail art" innovation. *Global Council for Restoration of the Earth's Environment* is designed to draw attention to the deterioration of St. Lucia's natural beauty.

Since the completion of this mammoth series – made entirely of recycled materials and carrying the seals and signatures of the world's largest environmental organisations and personalities – Xavier's work has taken on a new dimension of purity and depth.

He is currently working on a series of oils depicting a journey

through St. Lucian life. He is also experimenting with a variety of mediums, from acrylic paint to precious metals.

Llewellyn Xavier's highly versatile and valuable work can be viewed by appointment at his Cap Estate studio and also at his wife's gallery, St. Lucia Fine Art, at Pointe Seraphine.

He is known for his flamboyant oil paintings that successfully capture the colours and textures that are found throughout this stunning tropical island.

Left and above: Spectacular works of art by Llewellyn Xavier. Opposite Nobel Laureate Derek Walcott.

DEREK WALCOTT

St. Lucia's most respected playwright and poet, Derek Walcott won the Nobel Literature Prize in 1993. (It is believed that St. Lucia has produced more Nobel Laureates per capita than any other country in the world. Sir Arthur Lewis, a St. Lucian-born economist, won the Nobel Prize for Economics in 1979.)

Derek Walcott was born in St. Lucia in 1930. He was educated here and at the University of the West Indies in Jamaica, where he studied English, French and Latin. He studied theatre in New York and then went to live in Trinidad, where he worked as a full-time writer and dramatist. He founded the Trinidad Theatre Workshop and, between 1959 and 1979, wrote a number of impressive works that established him as a writer and dramatist.

He has taught English at the universities of Columbia, Yale, Harvard and Boston.

In 1988, he won the Queen's Medal for Poetry and, in 1993, he was deservedly awarded the Nobel Prize for Literature.

Dream on Monkey Mountain, *Ti Jean and his Brothers* and *Haytian Earth* are all dramatic works by

Walcott that have found audiences not only in the Caribbean but in the United States and the United Kingdom. His poetry collections include such acclaimed works as *In A Green Night*, *Omeros* and *The Arkansas Testament*.

His work is devoted to the Caribbean, and captures the spirit of the people and the beauty of the islands.

He now resides on a semi-permanent basis in St. Lucia, where he spends much time developing his brainchild, the Rat Island Foundation. Each year, the foundation brings a selected group of drama and literature students to St. Lucia to work during the summer vacation. At the end of this "summer school", the students then perform for the St. Lucian public.

LUTHER FRANÇOIS

From an early age, Luther François took violin lessons and soon learned to play virtually every instrument he touched. He went away to study music in Jamaica, however with his phenomenal talent and versatility he soon found himself teaching others rather than learning. Whilst in Jamaica, he was invited by reggae giants Bob Marley and Peter Tosh to accompany them on several recording sessions.

François began to experiment with a fusion of jazz and calypso music and became one of the exponents of calypso-jazz, – a new, sassy Caribbean beat. François is a founding member of the West Indies Jazz Band, a group of the finest jazz musicians in the Caribbean.

François, who also composes and arranges music, spends most of his time in Martinique, St. Lucia's neighbouring island. He is a modest man who is seemingly totally unaware of his incredible and colossal contribution to the sounds of Caribbean.

Whatever time of year you visit this magical island, you are always guaranteed a warm welcome and the promise of celebrations, for St.. Lucia boasts a calendar of festivities that stretches throughout the entire year.

Some have international appeal, some attract visitors from the Caribbean and others are strictly local affairs. Each festival has a different theme, and during nearly every month of the year, St. Lucians celebrate at least one special occasion.

Celebration of music

The **St. Lucia Jazz Festival**, which takes place every May, is by far the biggest event. It began in 1992 with world-renowned trumpeter Wynton Marsalis heading the musical line-up. However, due to a lack of pre-publicity, this three-day programme was more like a private party. All that soon changed and now the festival which is organised by the St. Lucia Tourist Board has become a well-attended week-long celebration. It is rated as one of the top five jazz events in the world. Enthusiasts descend on the island from across the Caribbean, the United States and

events

Europe to witness performances by some of the best musicians in the business.

The organisers match the style of the different musicians with appropriate settings. Evening concerts are held at the Castries Cultural Centre. Club-atmosphere performances take place at specially selected hotels. Out-of-town concerts are played in Vieux Fort, Soufrière and Laborie. "Jazz on the Square", a series of daily lunch-time performances, are held on Derek Walcott Square in central Castries.

Reserved for a weekend of open-air concerts is Pigeon Island – a striking setting with its green lawns sloping down towards the stage, juxtaposed perfectly with the sparkling blue of the Caribbean Sea. Performances begin in the early afternoon and it is dark by the time the four bands of the day finish their sets.

The music is a selection of cross-over and jazz fusion along with pure jazz to satisfy the tastes of the hard liners. For some visitors, the festival is an annual pilgrimage and the organisers aim to ensure thst everyone, including the musicians, have a good time. George Benson found his initial welcome so warm that he returned a second time. Among other performers who received a uniquely Caribbean welcome were George Duke, Carlos Santana, Tito Puente, Nancy Wilson and Earl Klugh. Caribbean musicians share the stage with the international guests. These include Luther François – St. Lucia's most talented musician, Len "Boogsy" Sharp from Trinidad and Arturo Tappin from Barbados.

Comedy and Christmas

Pigeon Island National Park is the venue for two other local festivals. The annual **Festival of Comedy** is hosted every April by the St. Lucia National Trust. This event brings together storytellers and comedians from all over the Caribbean, as well as St. Lucia. Non-stop, side-splitting performances are held either in the open-air at Pigeon Island or in the air-conditioned comfort of the Cultural Centre in Castries. Caribbean comedy often uses the form of storytelling and weaves a series of jokes around one long anecdote. St. Lucia's best-known raconteur, George "Fish" Alphonse, is a regular guest at this annual event.

He has created such personalities as "Country Boy", a young man in search of his roots, and "Grandpa", an old man who believes that an "old casserole makes the best soup" and that the aged have their contribution to make. "Fish" shares centre stage with people like Ken Crosbie from Barbados and Paul Keens-Douglas from Trinidad, the creator of the hilarious *Tantie Merle and Vibert*, stories.

In December, the St. Lucia National Trust in collaboration with the Folk Research Centre hold an annual **Christmas Folk Fiesta** at Pigeon Island. This is a celebration of a traditional Christmas in St. Lucia. There are Christmas personalities like Papa Jab and Toes and, of course, Santa Claus. Large quantities of traditional St. Lucian Christmas food and drink are also served.

Carnival time

Where would St. Lucia be without Carnival? The event used to be held during the traditional pre-Lenten period, two days before Ash Wednesday. However, the local Carnival committee, in conjunction with the St. Lucia Tourist Board, decided to transform the festival into a tourist attraction. As no-one in the Caribbean can begin to compete with the Carnival in

Trinidad and Tobago, the committee moved the date. **St. Lucia's Carnival** is now in July, but the high energy of the event remains the same.

In a bid to capture the calypso monarch crown, calypsonians spend the entire year studying current events and politics, and attempt to out-perform their contemporaries with the most satirical and comic compositions.

In the weeks leading up the to calypso finals, St. Lucia's best calypsonians – such as Herb Black, Ashanti, Lady Leen and Educator – present their new songs to local audiences. The public's reaction to the compositions is usually fairly indicative of how the judges will eventually vote. Costume designers search for the winning theme from which to create fantastic costumes to adorn their revellers and their candidates for the king and queen of the band competition. There is a carnival for children, and the Carnival Queen beauty contest selects the year's most beautiful young lady. During Carnival, an exciting mix of music which embraces calypso, steel pan, reggae and folk can be heard at parties around the island.

A year of festivites

St. Lucia's festival calendar is also dotted with several one-day celebrations. January, known as Nobel Laureate month, is when St. Lucia recognises the talents of its two Nobel Laureates – Derek Walcott and Sir Arthur Lewis, coincidentally both born on the 23rd. The government ministries of education and culture host a variety of literary and artistic events to mark the occasion.

On 22 February, St. Lucia celebrates the attainment of Independence – the island has been autonomous since 1979. Different activities are planned around **Independence Day**. One festival that is always a lively affair is the **Market Vendors' Feast**. Once farmers have grown the produce, it is left to the resourceful women to sell that produce in the market to supply the nation. On feast day, the market is gaily decorated and there is a competition to select the best stall. Music plays and liquor flows as these ladies ply their colourful wares. This is the ideal day to lunch in the market, as there is an abundance of delicious local food – both fresh and cooked – on sale.

The **Fisherman's Feast** is held in June on St. Peter's Day, the patron saint of fishermen. Professional fishing is a precarious and often unrewarding business, resulting in the occasional loss of life. Ironically, many St. Lucian fishermen do not know how to swim. Since the introduction of the outboard engine and larger fibreglass boats, fishermen's lives have been made slightly safer – but it is still a tough life. **St. Peter's Day** is the nation's way of paying homage to the patron saint of fishermen and acknowledging the efforts of the men who risk their lives on a daily basis. The day starts with a church service and then moves to the fishing ports, which have been decorated for the occasion. Here, the parish priest blesses the fishing crafts. The rest of the day is devoted to a lively party.

August begins with an occasion to reflect on serious issues. The first day of the month is **Emancipation Day**, recognising the 1838 abolition of slavery and the apprenticeship period which obliged ex-slaves to work on plantations without remuneration. The main event in the month, however, is the **Feast of St. Rose de Lima** on the 30th, run by the *La Rose Floral Society*. Its rival organisation, *La Marguerite*, holds its celebrations in October. *La Rose* and *La Marguerite* were initially secret societies started during the era of slavery. Seances invariably go on all night with performances of special songs, dances and ceremonies unique to each organisation. *La Rose*, the more flamboyant of the two societies, often opens its seances to the public.

Also in October, St. Lucia – along with all the Creole-speaking nations of the world, including Madagascar, Seychelles, Haiti, Martinique, Guadeloupe and Dominica – celebrates its special language. *Jounen Kweyol Etonasyonnal*, **International Creole Day**, is held towards the end of the month. In St. Lucia, the festival is organised by the Folk Research Centre. Every year, three villages are selected to host *Jounen Kweyol*. All aspects of the Creole culture are celebrated with traditional food and drink being served. Cultural performances of dancing and storytelling are held. Creole was once only a spoken language, but extensive work has been done to create a Creole orthography and a dictionary. The language is studied in universities and, as part of the *Jounen Kweyol* activities, Creolophone linguists and artists participate in symposiums on the language and cultures of the Creole nations.

St. Cecilia – the patron saint of musicians – is honoured at **The Musicians' Feast** in November. This occasion normally begins with a church service and is followed by special performances.

In addition to all these festivals, St. Lucia seems to have more public and bank holidays than any other country. As well as **New Year's Day**, St. Lucians also take 2 January as a holiday. **Independence Day** is, of course, a holiday, but so too is the 13 December, which is celebrated as **National Day**. It is believed to be the date when Christopher Columbus landed in St. Lucia and although historians are now fairly certain that Columbus never landed here, just in case, it remains a holiday! **Good Friday** and **Easter Monday** are both holidays, as is **Labour Day** on 1 May. In June, there is **Whitsuntide** weekend and **Corpus Christi.** Holidays in November include **All Saints and Remembrance Day**. At **Christmas** there are three official holidays. Sometimes these extra holidays fall on a Friday or on a Monday, making the weekend a deliciously long affair. The St.. Lucian people therefore have an additional fifteen days of fun and festivity in their annual calendar to celebrate the events that have shaped the island's history.

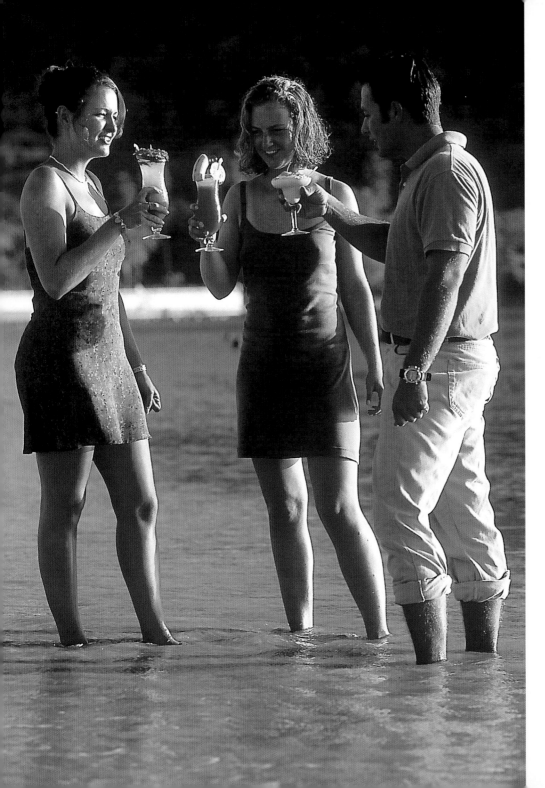

The dictionary describes the lime as a small green or yellow citrus fruit. But St Lucians have a very different definition. Mention a "lime" to an islander and they will get ready to party.

"Liming" is an integral part of the local lifestyle and means going to meet friends, making the rounds of other peoples' homes or simply checking out what is happening at the local bars and night-clubs.

St. Lucians have a plethora of places to "catch a lime." Long before the phrase became fashionable, St. Lucians – men in particular – frequented the island's rum shops. Every community has at least ten which are usually housed in small wooden buildings. Potent white rum is sold by the nip, half-nip or by the shot. The spirit is described as white but it is actually transparent and recommended only for the experienced rum drinker.

Those who cannot handle this fiery spirit drink ice-cold Piton beer – named after St. Lucia's most notable landmarks, as well as Heineken or Guinness.

In many rum shops, the game of dominoes is a regular fixture. The

get uncorked!

national domino team of St. Lucia has won many regional championships. Despite the fact that there is little physical activity involved, slapping dominoes is considered a national sport.

Nowadays, the rum shop is just one of many options for a lime as St. Lucia's bars come in a variety of shapes and sizes and from north to south everyone has their favourite.

Limers in search of a tranquil spot to enjoy a relaxing drink

make for Pigeon Island. The **Captain's Cellar** and *Jambe de Bois* are two peaceful bars and restaurants set in the neatly-manicured gardens and carefully-preserved ruins of St. Lucia's National Park. The sound of the sea gently lapping on the shore can be heard and it is an excellent venue for a full-moon lime.

The bars at the nearby **Hyatt Regency Hotel** have been incorporated into a series of meandering, man-made waterways and the hotel provides all the glamour of a first-class resort.

Towards Gros Islet and Rodney Bay, the lime becomes a more lively and upbeat affair. The tiny town of Gros Islet, St. Lucia's northernmost town, undoubtedly has more bars than anywhere else on the island.

Twenty years ago, Gros Islet was a quiet fishing village. Then the proprietor of **Scotty's Bar** began the tradition of barbecuing tender *lambi* (conch) brochettes served with an excellent spicy sauce. For the few select limers who had discovered Scotty's, Gros Islet became the place to start the weekend. The word gradually spread until Gros Islet became THE Friday night lime.

Nowadays, Friday night in Gros Islet involves the entire town. The main street and many side streets are closed to traffic and tables are set out along the road close to smoking barbecues which still offer *lambi* brochettes along with grilled chicken and fish. Cold beers and rum are the preferred beverages of the night

and bar staff have a full-time job on their hands just ensuring that the beers are adequately chilled. Conversation can be difficult as the hi-fi systems from the different establishments pump out the latest ragga, reggae and calypso and the main street becomes a vast dance floor.

At Rodney Bay Marina, a few hundred yards south of Gros Islet, the **Boatyard** at the dry dock, is a favourite watering hole for yachties from all over the world. **The Three Amigos**, at the Marina's jetty entrance, is an excellent Mexican restaurant that specialises in the finest margueritas in St. Lucia. It is a great place to lime.

Opposite: Holidaymakers enjoy tropical cocktails at sunset. Centre: Marigot Bay is a lively place to lime. Above: Sunshine, sand and a rum cocktail – total heaven.

Key Largo is a lively family-style pizzeria in Rodney Bay that serves great food and drinks.

Indies is just along from Key Largo. This discotheque, St. Lucia's largest, only opens on selected evenings and it is always full of hardened limers.

Most of St. Lucia's restaurants are concentrated in the Rodney Bay area. There is an excellent selection and wide choice of bars. **Snooty Agouti** is a bar and art gallery full of *objets d'art* and books to peruse. Jazz is the preferred music and a live band plays at least once a week. These sessions are sometimes broadcast live over the radio.

The **Triangle Pub** and the **Lime** are both open seven nights a week and, in addition to serving refreshing drinks, play non-stop ragga and calypso music. They

Above: A refreshing dip is even more pleasurable when enjoyed with an exotic cocktail. Right: There are countless rum shops scattered around St. Lucia.

also have an occasional steel band. Live entertainment is also provided at the weekly *Karaoke* nights (a passion among many St. Lucians).

Shamrock's Irish Pub is the place for live music, *Karaoke,* pool tables and fussball.

One of the most elegant spots, with its exotic cocktail list, is at the **Royal St. Lucian Hotel**. During the day hotel guests find their refreshments at the swim-up bar in the hotel's beautiful pool. Evenings in the stylish **Mistral Bar** are spent listening to jazz.

Spinnakers sits right on Reduit Beach, the most active liming beach in St. Lucia, while **Eagles' Inn** is at the end of the Rodney Bay Drive. Eagles' Inn has a pleasant bar and is set on the marina entrance in full view of arriving and departing yachts. At Bois d'Orange, at the turnoff for the Windjammer Hotel, **Laurel's Creole Restaurant and Bar** is a real, local lime, especially at lunch time on Saturday. **Windjammer Landing**

Resort has a great beach bar called **Jammers** that serves tasty bar food and imaginative cocktails. **Froggie Jacks** at the Vigie Marina, is a fabulous restaurant and bar set in a garden that overlooks the small inland sea.

Downtown Castries is active during the day, but as it is the business centre, few people have time to lime. Most bars offer a selection of refreshing, fresh fruit juices in addition to the strong stuff. A favourite local lime in town is **Kimlan's** on Derek Walcott Square. On Saturday, when the atmosphere is less business-like, a jazz ensemble plays during lunch at Kimlan's. After working hours, the city centre closes down and there are only few places to enjoy an evening drink.

Panache Café on Derek Walcott Square is two restaurants in one. The downstairs bistro offers an all-day buffet. The à la carte restaurant on the second floor is the only air-conditoned restaurant in Castries and serves excellent Caribbean and international cuisine. Live jazz performances are held each week and Café Panache has its own private club open to patrons and special members. One of the best spots is **Bam's Place** on the Chaussee Road. With its reputation for great local food, Bam's is also a place for an early lime (the bar closes at 10 pm) with friends.

People often like to lime out of town. In Marigot Bay, **J.J.'s Restaurant and Bar** is the Gros Islet alternative. On Wednesday, J.J. features a crab night. which is so popular that reservations are essential. J.J.'s also swings on Friday night. Open-air barbecues and street discos duplicate the Gros Islet lime, only on a smaller scale.

The bars in the west coast villages of Anse La Raye and Canaries, are mainly rum shops. At the entrance to the town of Soufrière is the **Hummingbird Restaurant and Bar**. The bar is a welcome stop off after a long drive.

The best way to visit the beach bar at **Anse Chastanet** is by a Soufrière water taxi from the town's jetty. The road to the hotel is otherwise terrible. South of Soufrière, on the road to Choiseul, is the turn off for the **Jalousie Hilton**, a fabulous resort nestled between the Pitons. However, a truly spectacular bar is at **Ladera,** further up the road.

Dasheene, the name of the resort's restaurant and bar, sits on a ridge below the summit of Petit Piton. There is nothing better than relaxing on this panoramic perch enjoying an exotic mix of local rum and fresh juices.

Between Soufrière and Laborie, there is a vast number of small bars and rum shops. This area is the home of some great country discos. The old-time establishments play an endless selection of country and western music, a form of music so popular that the annual country and western dance competition attracts participants from every corner of the island.

At the extreme south, in St. Lucia's second town, Vieux Fort, there are a couple of beach bars worth a visit. The **Reef**

Beach Café is the most popular beach bar in Vieux Fort. It sits right on the Anse de Sable beach, one of the most beautiful stretches of sand in St. Lucia. The Reef is open late. **Sandy Beach** at Anse de Sable is a lively bar and the local *Karaoke* spot..

There is a beach party nearly every weekend at Anse de Sable. Dance music, plenty of drink and delicious roasted corn are always on offer.

On St. Lucia, there are several floating bars, usually large catamarans, that offer daytime and moonlight cruises down St. Lucia's west coast. The cruise specialists who always sail with well-stocked bars are **Carnival Sailing, Cats** and the *Brig Unicorn*.

One word of caution; St. Lucians are serious limers, so be prepared to party until dawn!

From its broad fertile valleys intersected with sparkling rivers to secluded beaches fringed with graceful palms and the majestic Pitons that rise thousands of feet above the sea, St. Lucia must be one of the most enchanting islands to visit in the Caribbean. The natural beauty of this island has been a major influence in the architecture of the island's hotels which range from open-air rooms built around ancient trees to five-star luxury palaces sitting on golden sandy beaches. For additional information contact the St. Lucia Hotel and Tourism Association. (Tel: 758-452-5989/453-1811 Fax: 758-452-7967).

Anse Chastanet Hotel
PO Box 7000, Soufrière
Tel: 758-459-7000/7355
Fax: 758-459-7700
e-mail: ansechastanet@candw.lc

When architect Nick Troubetzkoy purchased this fabulous 600-acre plantation which surrounds the bay of Anse Chastanet about twenty-five years ago, it comprised of just a few octagonal gazebos scattered over a wooded hillside. He has since lovingly transformed this magical location into one of the most romantic holiday destinations in the world.

hang your hat

Troubetzkoy has travelled extensively and deplores the banality of top hotels around the world. His reaction has been to create a resort in which no two rooms are the same. Each of the hotel's forty-eight rooms is unique in its design and finish. The rooms are open and airy — many have only three walls, the fourth side being left completely open to the view. There is no air-conditioning, but all rooms have ceiling fans. Telephones are only found in the public areas and there is no television or radio to disturb the resort's peace and isolation.

Twelve units are located at beach level, while the rest of the cottages are dotted around the hillside overlooking the beach. The architecture is matchless and the use of local materials and craftsmanship in the furnishing and finish of the rooms completes an already perfect hideaway. Nick's wife, Karolin, looks after the marketing of Anse Chastanet with such success that the resort enjoys the highest rate of occupancy of any property on the island. It is often fully booked, so book well in advance.

The expansive views from the hillside are spectacular, with wide vistas across the sea and the rainforest-clad mountains to the Pitons beyond. The beach is undoubtedly one of the prettiest on the island – a crescent of dark volcanic sand fringed with graceful palms.

Charming and attentive staff cater to the needs of guests, serving cocktails in the two bars – one situated on the beach and the other up the hill near the main restaurant. Lunch is served in the beachside restaurant while breakfast and dinner are taken in the upper Pitons Restaurant.

While the accent is definitely on getting away from it all, there are also plenty of activities for guests at Anse Chastanet. The resort is in the heart of a protected Marine Reserve area and the snorkelling and Scuba diving are unparalleled with myriad corals, sponges and reef fish to be found just yards from the shore. The on-site dive operation, **Scuba St. Lucia**, provides masks and fins for snorkelling at no charge to hotel guests and also offers a full range of dive courses. These range from an introductory resort course up to certified instructor level. The courses are also conducted in a number of different languages.

Other watersports activities include kayaking, sunfish sailing and windsurfing. There is a tennis court at beach level, and a resident guide escorts more energetic guests on a variety of walks in the area, including to the nearby sands of Anse Mamin. A walk up the valley behind this beach leads to an old plantation, reservoir and watermill.

The charming *Kai Belte* (meaning "house of beauty") mini-spa is located directly on the beach where all guests are offered either a complimentary massage, manicure or facial on arrival. The spa offers a variety of excellent and beneficial treatments

Opposite and below: The outstanding resort of Anse Chastanet is quite unique. Many of the rooms have been constructed without a fourth wall to provide unrivalled vistas of the surrounding landscape.

Balembouche Estate
Choiseul
Tel: 758-455-1342

This delightful estate is located halfway between Choiseul and Laborie, near to Piage. A stay at Balembouche gives visitors the chance to experience a way of life that is virtually extinct elsewhere.

There is a pretty beach that can be reached by following the Balembouche River through the grounds for about ten minutes. The usually deserted bay is an ideal place to relax. The bedrooms in the main house are traditionally furnished with four-poster beds and the entire colonial-style building is furnished with antiques and *objets d'art* from a bygone era. Two comfortable estate cottages, each with two bedrooms, are located in the grounds.

A massive banyan tree dominates the gardens with shady branches spreading out over the lawns. The ruins of a sugar factory, complete with giant water-wheel and crushing mill, can be found in the grounds, along with a copper lime-oil still and other memorabilia of the past glories of the estate.

Tours of the estate are available to non-residents. (*see Sightseeing Spectacular page 49*).

Hummingbird Beach Resort
PO Box 280, Soufrière
Tel: 758-459-7232
Fax: 758-459-7033
e-mail: hbr@candw.lc

This charming resort has long been known to yachtsmen exploring the Caribbean. The well-appointed restaurant is open to the sea, offering beautiful views across the bay of Soufrière out to the Pitons beyond. It is decorated with local woodcarvings, pennants from visiting yachts and colourful batiks. It has twelve small, but well-ventilated rooms and most feature antique four-poster beds with mosquito nets. In the main building there are also two standard rooms with a shared bathroom, which is ideal for visitors on a budget.

The freeform pool is situated just above the beach, and although it is relatively small, it has the unusual features of a waterfall and rockery at one end.

The Hummingbird has gained a well-deserved reputation for good food over the years. The owner/manager, Joyce Alexander, offers a varied menu which combines West Indian, Asian and European dishes and the freshwater crayfish are a must whenever they are in season.

Jalousie Plantation Hilton Resort

Box 251, Soufrière
Tel: 758-459-7666
Fax: 758-459-7667

Located a mile south of Soufrière and overlooking the Pitons, the Jalousie Plantation is an idyllic and peaceful spot. This picture-book tropical setting with its own private bay conceals a comfortable and stylish hideaway.

Guests are accommodated in pretty villas which are scattered around the colourful gardens. All the rooms have air-conditioning and cable television, as well as a private plunge pool and patio. The sugar-mill roooms are located in a wing near the centre of the complex and provide the advantage of being within easy walking distance of most public areas and restaurants.

Visitors looking for a change from rest and relaxation are offered a wide range of activities and excursions. Island tours, a variety of watersports, golf or tennis are available; and there is a pool situated beside the beachfront bar where guests can enjoy delicious grills and snacks. Experienced or first-time divers can also indulge in snorkelling and diving amongst the dazzling reef fish and corals.

Ladera Resort

PO Box 225, Soufrière
Telephone: 758-459-7323
Fax: 758-459-5156
e-mail: reservations@ladera-stlucia.com

Over the last twenty-five years, the small town of Soufrière has become synonymous with exceptional hotels. It is possible that the catalyst for this trend dates back to the unparalleled vision of John DiPol, a brilliant American architect who first visited St. Lucia in the 1960s to design and build the apartments which made up the original Dasheene property. DiPol has recently returned to the island to oversee a major extension and renovation of this outstanding

resort and all the new units will be fashioned in the same unique style as the original development.

Ladera is situated just 2 miles (3.5km) from Soufrière up a steep hill overhung with lush rainforest and tropical flora. The property is quite extraordinary – nestling 1,000 feet (305 metres) above sea level on the verdant ridge that runs between the volcanic Pitons.

The buildings are constructed from green heart, a South American wood, as well as from local woods and stone. They are

Opposite: The elegant interior of the Balembouche Estate. Above: The fabulous Jalousie Hilton sits in the shadow of Gros and Petit Piton.

Whilst totally private and entirely sheltered from the elements, the design gives the illusion of living in a luxurious tree house.

In total there are twenty-four accommodation "units", comprising eighteen suites and six villas. The suites, all of which have an open-air bedroom, range from one-bedroom suites to two-bedroom suites with a large plunge pool. For larger families or groups, there are six different villas – most equipped with private pools – dotted around the estate. These have both open-air and enclosed bedrooms. Every room has been individually designed and all the polished wooden furniture is locally crafted. The carved four-poster beds in the main bedrooms are particularly impressive. The floors are terra cotta with colourful mosaic inserts and the walls are hung with attractive local paintings. Each private outdoor living room faces the Pitons. The bathrooms incorporate unique natural features such as conch shells as faucets. There are no telephones

or television to disturb the tranquillity of this idyllic location.

The main pool is designed with a vanishing edge on the western side to allow unobstructed views of the Pitons. The pool deck is bordered with magnificent terraced gardens that lead down the Soufrière valley side of the property and provide peaceful walks amidst exotic flowering trees and shrubs.

The bar and restaurant overlook the pool and the theme of woodcarving continues – most notably in the striking frieze around the bar itself. The open-air *Dasheene* restaurant affords the same spectacular view as the rest of the property and is refreshingly cool even on the hottest nights. Magnus Alnabeck, the resort's charming and knowledgeable manager, is justifiably proud of the many awards and commendations that the restaurant has received for its creative and innovative menu over the years.

This is a resort for the romantic, the artist, the nature lover and anyone looking to escape from reality. On an island which features a number of small resorts, Ladera is the undoubted jewel in the crown.

perched at the edge of the ridge that drops precipitously to Jalousie beach far below. The views are spectacular – particularly at sunset when the sun drops directly between the Pitons into the Caribbean Sea. To take full advantage of the view each villa and suite has been designed with an open fourth wall on the western side of the hotel.

Above: The dazzling pool at Ladera sits high in the mountains overlooking the Pitons and Jalousie beach below.

La Haut Plantation

PO Box 304, Soufrière
Tel: 758-459-7008
Fax: 758-459-5975
e-mail: allainj@candw.lc

This hotel was built originally as the private home for owners Joe and Stephanie Allain. However, the location proved so popular with their friends that they were persuaded to open it to the public as a restaurant and bar. The Allains have since expanded the property to include five guest bedrooms, a small cottage, a sports bar and swimming pool.

La Haut Plantation is set into the hillside about two miles north of Soufrière on the road to Castries. For anyone on a budget, this is an ideal spot. The bedrooms in the main block are built in the style of a plantation house and the white walls are accented with blue and mauve woodwork. They have high ceilings and enjoy cooling breezes from the surrounding rainforest. Most have king-size beds and ensuite bathrooms.

The restaurant serves delicious dishes that include many of the fresh fruits and vegetables grown on the plantation itself. The sports bar has a satellite dish and a large-screen television. For visitors interesting in walking, La Haut Plantation makes an ideal base camp as it is situated high on the ridge that overlooks Soufrière and the Pitons. Seek some local advice or hire a guide before starting off and enjoy some spectacular hikes or walks in the area.

Mago Estate Hotel

Soufrière
Tel: 758-459-7352
Fax: 758-459-7359

Mago Estate sits on a steep hillside overlooking Soufrière. Built originally as a private house by an eccentric German developer, the property is exceptional. There are just five bedrooms – each named after a Roman emperor. They are all beautifully furnished and have an open side that faces the town and Pitons in the distance.

The public areas are extraordinary and the overall feeling is one of camping without any of the inconvenience. The restaurant is carved directly into the hillside some 20 feet (6 metres) above the pool and each table enjoys the full splendour of the view. The comfortable living room features a massive volcanic rock that thrusts into the room with a large open fireplace set into its base. A magnificent mango tree grows in the centre of the room and a small tree house nestles in its branches.

The entire structure seems to have grown out of the hillside – rocks protrude at random in the bedrooms, trees continue to grow in and around the buildings and the entire property is adorned with allamanda, bougainvillaea and many other tropical plants.

The restaurant is under the capable control of the ebullient manager Monica Lenihan and entrées change each evening. The cuisine is generally French with strong flavours and influences from the Caribbean. A weekly barbeque is cooked in the main fireplace and served to the mellow sounds of local musicians. There is a wonderful feeling of space about Mago and this is definitely the spot for those who enjoy small and unusual properties and revel in being close to nature and all its bounties.

Stonefield Estate
PO Box 228, Soufrière
Tel: 758-459-5530/7037
Fax: 758-459-5550

Spacious and beautifully decorated, the Stonefield Estate is a delightful place to enjoy a stay on St. Lucia. Just south of Soufrière, and sitting almost in the shadow of Petit Piton, the Stonefield Estate was once a cocoa plantation. The original plantation buildings have since been converted into elegantly-furnished villas, all of which have spectacular views. Malgretoute Beach is only a fifteen-minute walk away and there is a courtesy shuttle service provided by the hotel. Each villa has been individually designed to

Above: The peaceful setting of the Marigot Beach Club.

harmoniously blend with the charming architectural style of the original property. The villas, each furnished with exquisite antique hand-made furniture, have a bedroom, bathroom, living and dining area, fully-equipped kitchen and veranda. Some villas also have an outdoor, but nevertheless totally private, shower. There is a resident housekeeper who supervises the running of the premises and the services of a cook can be provided by prior arrangement.

Marigot Beach Club
PO Box 101, Marigot Bay
Tel: 758-451-4974
Fax: 758-451-4973
e-mail: mbc@candw.lc

This new resort has thirty-two studio apartments and villas dotted around Marigot Bay.

Every room has a ceiling fan, bathroom and private patio; and the villas each have a kitchenette. Good food is always available in *Doolittles*, a waterfront restaurant named after the film that was shot in this tropical location. The menu offers a selection of Caribbean,as well as continental dishes, to guests and the many visitors from the yachts that are an ever-changing feature of the Bay.

Bay Gardens Hotel
P.O. Box 1892, Castries
Tel: 758-452-8060
Fax: 758-452-8059
e-mail: baygardens@candw.lc

This intimate award-winning hotel is a great find in the heart of Rodney Bay, just ten minutes stroll from Reduit Beach. There is a wonderful warmth to the staff who get to know all the guests by name during their stay. There are few hotels that can compete with the charm of the management team which is headed up by Berthia and Johnnie Parle.

All the spotless pastel-coloured rooms are furnished in white wicker and come with terraces or balconies that overlook the lush gardens with its pools, jacuzzi and waterfalls. Each room is air-conditioned and equipped with television, refrigerator and radio.

The pleasant *Spices Restaurant* is good value, and the *Cinnamon Bar and Lounge* is a delightful haven to relax and enjoy a cocktail after a long day in the sun.

Royal St. Lucian Hotel

Reduit Beach,
PO Box 977, Castries
Tel: 758-452-9999
Fax: 758-452-9639

At the northern end of St. Lucia, the magnificent Royal St. Lucian sits in splendour on the golden sands of Reduit Beach.

The imposing palazzo-style reception area sets the style for this grand hotel. Each of its ninety-six luxuriously-appointed suites are a fine example of architectural innovation which is both practical and imaginative. They all feature a bedroom with either a king-size or twin beds, a separate living room, luxurious marble bathroom and a patio or balcony offering spectacular views of the gardens or sea. There is also a telephone, safe, minibar, hairdryer, cable television and radio. The bedrooms are slightly raised from the living area and concealed at night behind flowing drapes and shutters. There are also eight oceanfront suites with expansive terraces that sit directly above the beach.

The Presidential Suite, as befits its title, combines all the features of the standard suites, but has the added luxury of an outdoor jacuzzi on its own private terrace.

The hotel sits in beautifully manicured grounds which include a landscaped pool with a swim-up bar. More active outdoor pursuits and sports can be arranged through the helpful staff on the front-desk and include horseback riding, waterskiing, deep-sea fishing as well as snorkelling Scuba diving and golf.

The fabulous Royal Spa offers massage, reflexology and body wraps as well as a range of beauty treatments. There is also a fitness centre with a jacuzzi, sauna and steam room located within the Royal Spa and personal trainers are on hand to recommend the most suitable exercise programmes for all levels of fitness.

Above and left: The elegant reception area and pool at the Royal St. Lucian Hotel.

Guests are also offered excellent choice of casual or formal dining. (*See Eat Your Heart Out, page 142*).

The hotel is run by the charming softly-spoken Alan Hunter, a veteran of the hotel industry for over thirty years. His standards for excellence are reflected throughout the property in concert with a dedicated team of delightful and loyal staff. Requests for assistance are always met with a genuine desire to ensure that guests are guaranteed a stress-free stay. It is telling to watch Mr. Hunter and his staff bid tearful guests a fond farewell at the end of their stay to know that despite the opulence and sophistication of this hotel, guests are cossetted in an environment of genuine hospitality and affection.

Rex St. Lucian Hotel
Reduit Beach,
PO Box 512, Castries
Tel: 758-452-8351
Fax: 758-452-8331

An ideal family resort, the Rex St. Lucian boasts an excellent location on the sands of Reduit Beach. The airy lobby leads to the lush tropical gardens and swimming pool, as well as directly to the beach. The 120 rooms are laid out over two floors and all are furnished with Caribbean-style rattan furniture and double or king-size beds. They are equipped with air conditioning, shower, bath and cable television, as well as a hairdryer and safe.

For meals, guests can choose between the beachside *Mariners* restaurant where the fare ranges from simple sandwiches and snacks to hearty buffets; or the elegant air-conditioned *Oriental*. (*See Eat Your Heart Out, page 142*).

There are lighted tennis courts for matches in the cool of the evening and various watersports are available on the beach at a nominal charge.

Above: One of the elegant suites in the Royal St. Lucian Hotel. Left: A multitude of bubbles in the Presidential Suite's outdoor jacuzzi!

East Winds Inn

Labrelotte Bay,
PO Box 1477, Castries
Tel: 758-452-8212
Fax: 758 452 9941

Located on Labrelotte Bay to the north of Castries, East Winds is a perfect beachside hideaway. The resort has only thirty rooms located in beautifully-maintained grounds shaded by giant bamboo and mango trees.

The rooms all have a king-size bed, telephone, safe, hairdryer, ceiling fan, coffee and tea-making facilities and a mini bar, which is re-stocked daily. The cottages that made up the original hotel feature elegant rattan furniture and wooden louvered windows. Each has a terra cotta brick patio and padded bench seating shaded by a thatched rondavelle.

The eight superior units are a recent addition to the property and have been fashioned as Caribbean-style cottages with two rooms per unit. They are decorated in pastel shades and are spacious and airy. The rooms have cable television, radio and video, along with remote-controlled ceiling fans. A mini-bar and coffee-making facilities are situated outside on the balcony. Each cottage is surrounded by lush vegetation providing a real sense of privacy. A short walk from the bedrooms leads past the freeform pool with its self-service swim-up bar. Tea, coffee and cakes are served here each afternoon.

The charming open-air restaurant is one of the most magical locations on the island. It is here that Chef Frank Chevrier works his culinary genius to produce memorable dishes that utilize the very best of the island's produce. The clubhouse is situated behind the restaurant. Complete with its own small bar it provides comfortable and relaxed seating in an elegant open-air setting.

East Winds is, without doubt, one of St. Lucia's most lovely hotels. The combination of its intimate setting and personable service leave guests feeling rejuvenated and refreshed after their stay.

Le Sport

Cariblue Beach,
PO Box 437, Castries
Tel: 758-450-8551
Fax: 758-450-0368

Situated at the northern tip of the island, this luxurious all-inclusive spa hotel offers everything for the world-weary executive. Le Sport is dedicated to every aspect of a "Body Holiday" and offers fabulous facilities and treatments for both mental and physical relaxation.

The 102 rooms are all decorated in pastel colours and equipped with air-conditioning, refrigerators, radios and hair-dryers. Most of the rooms have ocean views and all have private terraces or patios. The hotel also offers unusual accommodation in *Manderley*, a Victorian-style plantation house set within a delightful tropical garden. This three-bedroom gingerbread house is decorated with period antiques and offers spectacular views of the island. The house also includes a comfortable living room, library, private pool and a terrace where staff serve breakfast every morning.

Left: The open-air restaurant at the East Winds Inn is one of the most beautiful settings for dinner on St. Lucia.

For the energetic guest, there is a wide selection of regular resort activities including snorkelling, Scuba diving, waterskiing, windsurfing, tennis, cycling and volleyball. Visitors who enjoy variety in their leisure activities can try their skills at archery, fencing, croquet and table tennis. There is also complimentary access to a nearby nine-hole golf course on the Cap Estate where the green fees are included in the cost of the holiday.

The Oasis is the resort's treatment spa which is housed in a Moorish-style mini-palace surrounded by lily-ponds and fountains. A variety of superb treatments are available, including aromatherapy and Swedish massages, reflexology, body scrubs, facials and hair treatments. There are also algae bubble baths, seaweed wraps and jet showers. Guests can also try a course of Tao Chi or yoga, or join the regular fitness classes.

The spa also has a Clarins Institute de Beauté, which offers treatments using the all-natural products from this well-known French company.

Unique among luxury all-inclusive resorts, Le Sport combines the pleasures of an active beach vacation with programmes designed to revitalise and relax both body and mind.

Sandals St. Lucia La Toc
PO Box 399, Castries
Tel: 758-452-3081
Fax: 758-452-1012
e-mail: sandals@candw.lc

One of the world's most glamorous all-inclusive resorts – Sandals St. Lucia La Toc defies description. From the lavish lobby to the romantic villa suites with their own private plunge pools, five gourmet dining rooms, three pools, seven bars, its own nine-hole golf course, floodlit tennis courts and state-of-the-art health spa – nothing has been spared to create one of the most impressive all-inclusive resorts in the Caribbean.

All the rooms are furnished in dark mahogany and feature king-size four-poster beds. Air conditioning, cable television, direct-dial phones and hair-dryers are standard; and the suites have a concierge service. Accommodation is provided for guests with disabilities and the hotel staff can provide further details on the facilities available.

Virtually every sport and recreation is provided including waterskiing, shuffleboard, Scuba diving, windsurfing and croquet.

After dark, entertainment can be found in the nightclub or piano bar. There is also a courtesy shuttle service to the excellent Sandals Halcyon located on the beachfront at Choc Bay, a few miles away. Guests at both Sandals resorts can use the facilities at either hotel at no extra cost.

Left: Guests at Le Sport are offered a variety of sporting activities including golf at a nearby nine-hole course on the Cap Estate. Opposite: Villas dot the hillside at the Windjammer Landing Resort.

Windjammer Landing Resort

Labrelotte Bay,
PO Box 1504, Castries
Tel: 758 452 0913
Fax: 758 452 9454

This beautiful resort was built by the renowned British architect Ian Morrison and offers a variety of facilities to suit the need of every traveller. Many of the 200 rooms in this Mediterranean-style condominium village have plunge pools and every room is furnished with characteristic plantation-style rattan furniture. Some of the larger units also have a small, but fully-equipped kitchen. Every condominium overlooks the sea and each bedroom has access to a private terrace.

Terra cotta pathways thread through the lush gardens and link the bedrooms to the resort's main facilities which include a wide choice of restaurants and bars. The plantation house, which overlooks Labrelotte Bay, contains the *Mango Tree* restaurant which offers great food in a relaxed atmosphere. For more authentic, local cooking, *Josephine's* serves Caribbean and Creole dishes in an open-air setting. Fresh salads, snacks and drinks are available around the clock in the timber-and-thatch *Jammers Restaurant and Bar*.

The *Brick-Oven* is the place to sample delicious Greek and Italian dishes, as well as authentic pizza.

In addition to the four freshwater pools, there are floodlit tennis courts and a full range of watersports including snorkelling, windsurfing, water-skiing and banana boat rides.

Villas

A tropical villa in St. Lucia offers privacy and freedom in a luxurious environment. Villa rentals on St. Lucia range from one to six bedrooms and most of them are set in landscaped gardens in the hills of Cap Estate. Others are located in Rodney Bay, the Vigie Peninsula and in Soufrière. All have private swimming pools with the exception of the townhouses in Rodney Bay which share a large pool. All villas and townhouses are fully self-contained and staffed. Most of the housekeepers are excellent cooks and are also happy to help with shopping.

A particular favourite is *La Paloma Villa* which is conveniently located in a private residential area of Vigie. This enchanting property features an eclectic mix of Caribbean and Mexican furnishings. Antique Mexican doors lead to a terra cotta courtyard with a sparkling fountain. A spacious terrace runs the length of the property and leads to the lush tropical gardens and freshwater swimming pool.

Tropical Villas St. Lucia have a wide range of rentals available throughout the year. They can be contacted on Tel: 758-450-8240/0349. Fax: 450 8089. e-mail: tropvil@candw.lc.

eat your

heart out!

St. Lucia is peppered with some of the best restaurants in the Caribbean. Their chefs have taken the best of West Indian cooking – with its exotic spices, fruits, vegetables, and seafood – and added a soupçon of European techniques to produce a sophisticated and modern Caribbean cuisine. The result is one of the most sensual experiences of the islands.

The first settlers on St. Lucia were the Arawaks and Caribs, native Indians from South America, and they introduced the cassava plant, a West Indian staple and the basic ingredient of the hot sauce in the legendary pepperpot stew. The dish was originally created by the Arawak farmers, who, having spent long hours in the fields, had little time to prepare meals. A stew of several meats with plenty of vegetables and black pepper was put on to simmer at the beginning of the day. By dusk the workers were able to enjoy this thick, hearty soup. Today's version uses chicken, lamb, beef and pork instead of the original Amerindian recipe which included agouti, iguana and opossum!

Left The elegant interior of the Oriental Restaurant is another world dominated by the ambience and flavours of the east.

The pepperpot was kept warm overnight and the next day further provisions added so the dish was sometimes kept hot for weeks at a time. The juice of the cassava – known as *casareep* – provided the hot seasoning in the pepperpot. There is a poison which has to be first extracted from the cassava and it is possible that any traces of poison in the spicy dish worked as a preservative and kept the ever-boiling pot safe for human consumption. In today's kitchens the pot is only boiled for a day instead of several weeks, but the custom of adding any available ingredients still applies. This delicious dish is served with small flour dumplings or rice.

Local cuisine makes use of an interesting mix of native crops and imports. Banana, plantain, sugar and pineapple were introduced in the 15th century by the Spanish and today these tasty crops are a mainstay of an islander's diet.

African slaves brought over seeds of vegetable and fruit crops, such as okra, yams and pigeon peas. Pigeon peas are also known as red peas or gungo peas, and they are the main ingredient of a local dish known simply as "rice and peas", which is served with a splash of hot pepper sauce.

Spices distinguish Caribbean cooking perhaps more than anything else. Hot pepper sauces join the salt and pepper on every St. Lucian dining table. Ginger, pimento and nutmeg are also favourite seasonings.

Be sure to sample the wonderful local breads, such as banana or pumpkin bread. Roti is an Indian creation which is available everywhere – it is a paper-thin dough wrapped round a spicy curry mixture of either meat, chicken or fish (ask for one without bones, which the locals like to chew on!).

When the European settlers came to the Caribbean islands the French developed the zesty Creole sauce using tomatoes – already being grown by the Indians – combined with onions, celery, garlic, hot peppers and parsley.

Fruits of the ocean

Surrounded by the sea, seafood dishes are predictably the main specialities. Check menus for large game fish, such as swordfish, marlin, kingfish and mahi-mahi – its local name is dorado or dolphin – so don't call for Greenpeace

The whole of the Caribbean is justly famous for its tropical fruits, such as mango, banana, pineapple, papaya, passion fruit, lime and many more. They are particularly satisfying when made into a refreshing ice cream, milkshake or a cooling fruit punch.

Various international cuisines exist alongside the local cooking. Visitors can choose from Chinese, Indian, French and Italian. Many hotels offer exotic buffet dinners and barbecues – fiery hot sauce can be added at your peril!

Dining out is a relaxed pastime in St. Lucia and few restaurants have a dress code. Lunches are often eaten at beach cafés. Most restaurants provide good service, but without the sense of urgency you might find at home – so sit back, relax and treat yourself to another cocktail while soaking up the atmosphere.

Many restaurants are often busy and some close on one night during the week. Most establishments accept both Visa and MasterCard, but check on other types of credit card. Few restaurants stay open much later

when you see "dolphin" on the menu! Tuna and the tasty red snapper are also widely available. Coconut cream is a favourite sauce for fish. Conch, or *lambi*, may be deep-fried as fritters, steeped in chowder, or barbequed on the side of the road. Boiled crabs, spicy stuffed land crabs and even sea urchins are favourite snacks. The St. Lucian national fish dish is "green fig and salt fish". This is a delicious combination of unripe green bananas cooked with cured salty cod, flavoured with sautéed herbs in coconut oil.

than 11.00pm due to the lack of public transport for staff late at night. It is advisable to make reservations, particularly during the high season.

Drinks

Exotic fruit punches and rum-based cocktails are the true taste of the Caribbean, so while you are in St. Lucia treat yourself to a drop of the national tipple. Most bars have their own speciality and an extensive list of creative cocktails. (*See Where to Get Uncorked, page 124*). The famous *pina colada* (pineapple, coconut cream and rum) or the *daiquiri* (crushed ice, rum and fruit syrup) are definitely worth sampling, along with the ubiquitous "rum punch". Non-alcoholic fruit punches are delicious too, and the combinations are endless.

Another option available in St. Lucia is fresh coconut, often sold on the street. Don't be alarmed if you are greeted by the vendor wielding a machete – it is simply used to chop the top off the coconut. Choose an older coconut if you can, because the milk is sweeter.

Sugar molasses is the inspiration behind rum. Fifty years ago bars kept their bottles of rum on the counter for consumption free of charge – customers just had to pay for the water. Times have obviously changed in terms of complimentary libation, but there is still a huge variety of rum to choose from. White rum is the preferred local tipple, but darker rum, coloured with caramel in the ageing processis also widely available. After dinner, mature and vintage rums are served as a *digestif*, like European brandy.

The locally-produced Piton beer is extremely refreshing – particularly when served ice-cold. It is one of the tastiest beers in the Caribbean and a definite thirst quencher for those who have endured a busy day of relaxing in the sunshine! A good selection of wines is available, but they can be quite expensive because of high import taxes. Chilean and Californian wines tend to be more reasonably priced and make an excellent alternative to the more pricey European brands. Tap water is safe to drink, as are the ice cubes made from it, although mineral water is widely available for those in doubt.

The best advice for dining in St. Lucia? Be bold and try some of the local dishes, try something like curried chicken served in a coconut shell, or curried goat. If you wish to try authentic Caribbean cuisine, St. Lucia offers a huge range of restaurants to suit all tastes and pockets. You will be sure to enjoy some memorable meals that are unique to this enchanted isle.

Bon Appetit!

The Great House Restaurant
Cap Estate
Tel: 450-0450
Fax: 450-0451

The Great House is an elegant mix of French and Creole styles. The stone building was constructed on the foundations of the original De Longueville House, one of the first estate houses on the island. This is a superb setting for dinner where the elegant dining room recreates the atmosphere of a bygone era. There is an excellent fixed-price four course menu, or an equally delicious à la carte selection that includes many vegetarian dishes. The peerless Great House Restaurant lives up to its name in every way – the service is excellent and the food is a stylish blend of Mediterranean, modern European and Caribbean cuisine using high quality ingredients.

Opposite: Sparklingly-fresh fruits of the ocean. Below: The wide shady terrace at the Great House Restaurant overlooks beautiful grounds.

L'Epicure

The Royal St. Lucian Hotel
Tel: 452-9999
Fax: 452-9639

The magnificent Royal St. Lucian is a luxury hotel situated on the sands of Reduit Beach. Within its grounds is L'Epicure is a sophisticated bar and restaurant with a terrace that overlooks the gardens and shimmering waters of the Caribbean Sea. Its elegant bar is an airy and relaxing venue for pre- and post-dinner drinks, which are served to the gentle sounds of a classical or jazz pianist. When you are ready to dine, the delicious menu has a strong French flavour and the service is impeccable. Seafood being a speciality, try the Creole-style lobster, simmered in onions, paprika, parsley and white wine, in a tomato-based sauce and presented in the shell. The warm Caribbean freshwater shrimps presented in a garlic and citrus butter served on a bed of seasonal leaves or stuffed loin of lamb roasted in a red wine and thyme jus with a hint of teriyaki

Top: Tuna sashimi is served with a delicious blend of wasabi and soy sauce. Centre: L'Epicure in the Royal St. Lucian Hotel is renowned for its delicious fresh lobster. Bottom: Tasty mussels in garlic butter at the Coal Pot Restaurant. Opposite: The quaint interior of the Coal Pot Restaurant at Vigie.

sauce set on a sweet potato rosti are two other dishes which give this outstanding restaurant its well-deserved reputation. The wine list is unrivalled on the island and is also one of the best in the Caribbean. Some nights of the week have a special theme – so check when making a reservation. A particular favourite is the enchanting weekly beach dinner served on the sands of Reduit Beach beneath the stars.

The Oriental

Located off the Admiral's Lounge
Rex St. Lucian Hotel
Tel: 452-8351

When you pass the lions guarding the entrance to the Oriental, make a wish for good luck, as they do in China. Inside the restaurant you are transported into another world dominated by the ambience and flavours of the east. The milieu is enhanced by the wafting strains of gentle sitar music and the heady aroma emanating from the huge black-lacquered incense burner which dominates the centre of the room. The head chef, Adil Sherwani, formerly of the Taj Hotel in Bombay, has created an intriguing menu combining influences from India, China, Thailand and Japan. The sashimi, a delicious mix of raw local fish accompanied by wasabi and soy sauce is a must, as is the zesty beef pepper salt, or the dim sum selection. There is a wide selection of entrées from which to choose, including the mouthwatering tandoori chicken, or the chilli bean fish – a delicious blend of local fish flavoured with fresh herbs and spices. The succulent sweet-and-sour pork is highly recommended, as is the Thai-style prawn, delicately seasoned with lemon grass, coconut and ginger. In classic eastern style, the service attentive, but unobtrusive. A superb wine list compliments this blend of international flavours.

La Nautique
The Royal St. Lucian Hotel
Tel: 452-9999
Fax: 452-9639

La Nautique is a delightful open-air poolside restaurant at the elegant Royal St. Lucian Hotel. Guests are invited to create their own fabulous breakfast from the buffet which offers an incredible choice of cold meat, cheese, pastries, breads, tropical fruits and juices, as well a delicious selection of hot dishes. Lunch is served here and the menu is essentially gourmet European with a Caribbean flair. It combines an excellent selection of locally-grown and imported produce, all served in a classical, but innovative style. The fresh hot soups made from local breadfruit or pumpkin and the delicious Caesar salads are particularly worthy of note. Guests may choose from the full à la carte menu, tasty snacks or the low-fat Spa menu. Whatever your choice La Nautique caters for every taste and health regime.

The Coal Pot
Vigie Marina
Castries
Tel: 452-5566

This delightful open-air restaurant is situated on the waterfront at Vigie Marina. The Coal Pot is run by its French chef Xavier who produces some innovative and highly-assured cooking. His delightful St. Lucian wife, Michelle is responsible for the dazzling Caribbean landscapes which decorate the walls. The food is contemporary Caribbean and seafood figures prominently. The menu which demonstrataes some well-judged flavour combinations changes daily and includes dishes such as local crab back, *callaloo* soup, mussels in garlic butter, all served with imaginative salads and delicious local vegetables. The wine list is drawn from France, Italy and California and provide an exciting and varied choice to suit every palette.

Plantation Restaurant
Jalousie Hilton Resort
Tel: 459-7666

The location of this charming restaurant makes a striking impact on newcomers and the food continues to impress. Set in the valley between the magnificent Pitons, the colonial-style Plantation Restaurant is elegant and airy. The contemporary menu is inspired by flavours taken from around the globe and the wine list is excellent. This is a beautiful setting for diners looking for a magical evening.

Memories of Hong Kong
Rodney Bay
Tel: 452-8218

This is an authentic Cantonese restaurant where the proprietor, Yee, has successfully re-created the essence and flavour of Hong Kong. The hinged, wooden shutters open up to allow the warm night breeze to filter into the restaurant's interior, where the vibrant red and black decor is lit by oriental lanterns. The crispy Peking duck is excellent, and is served with pancakes and plum sauce. The menu promises freshly-caught seafood served in garlic, yellow bean or black bean sauce, as well as chicken, meat and vegetable dishes. Many traditional Chinese favourites are available including bird's nest soup. The service is friendly and the wine list well priced.

Razmataz Tandoori Restaurant
Rodney Bay
Tel: 452-9800
Fax: 452-9800

Razmataz is one of the best Indian restaurants in the Caribbean. It is centrally located, just opposite the Royal St. Lucian Hotel in Rodney Bay. The faultless charm of the staff, courteous good humour and luxuriant setting combine to make this one of the most sensational dining experiences on the island. The charming Nepalese chef, Dependra, creates mouthwatering meat or fish selections with an original and innovative blend of Indian spices. The menu offers a fabulous variety of authentic dishes, ranging from mild *korma* to hot *vindaloo*. The complex blend of vegetables and spices which make up some of the vegetarian dishes are unique and the use of local produce adds a new dimension to an unforgettable Indian meal. The ambience is regularly enhanced by the proprietor John Wright who performs some golden oldies to the delight of his diners.

Capone's Restaurant
Rodney Bay
Tel: 452-0284
Fax: 452-3264

Capone's is a traditional taste of the best of Italy and diners can be sure of a warm welcome from the charming proprietress, Sharman Hamber. The restaurant is an elegant blend of art deco and contemporary design with a cool and relaxing atmosphere. The chef combines an innovative mix of Mediterranean herbs with either fish or meat to create some delicately-flavoured dishes, although you can order a delicious, but spicy, chicken piri-piri. For dessert, try the superb banoffee pie and complete your meal with one of their liqueur coffees. In keeping with the restaurant's 1930s Chicago gangster theme, the bill comes in a violin case.

Capone's – La Piazza
Tel: 452-0284

Capone's garden dining area is a lively place where fresh pizza and steaming hot pasta dishes are the most popular dishes. However, there is also a demand for the excellent beef pepperpot, tasty barbecued steaks, grilled chicken and fish. This is a fun, Italian-style family restaurant.

Froggie Jack's

Vigie Cove
Tel: 458-1900
Fax: 458-2911

Froggie Jack's restaurant and cocktail bar is located five minutes from the centre of Castries. The sophisticated elegance of this waterside location set amidst lush tropical gardens provides a picture-perfect setting to enjoy a meal which is guaranteed to surpass all expectations. French owner and chef Jacky Rioux has created an contemporary menu that successfully juxtaposes culinary cultures and flavours from the Mediterranean and the islands of the Caribbean. The restaurant enjoys a fine reputation for its seafood dishes, in particular the squid in a lime and chive sauce served in a filo pastry basket, or the delicious mixed fish and seafood soup. A feeling of confidence underlies such dishes as king prawns in garlic and ginger as well as the pan-seared king scallops in a tomato and ginger butter. Other dishes to try are the succulent rack of lamb with mustard sauce or classic beef fillet in a green peppercorn and brandy sauce. An excellent selection of wines compliments this great menu.

Bon Appetit Restaurant

Morne Fortune
Tel: 452-2757

Bon Appetit offers a fabulous night-time view across Castries, and on a clear night as far as Martinique. There are only five tables in this intimate restaurant, so book in advance. The delightful hosts, Sheri and Renato Venturi, create delicious home-made soups and appetizers and serve their speciality – freshwater crayfish – with pride. The menu is simple, but offers enough variety to suit all tastes. This small guesthouse is filled with comfortable antique furniture creating a colonial atmosphere, and the walls are decorated with Sheri's hand-painted tropical artwork.

Rain Restaurant

Brazil Street
Castries
Tel: 452-1515

Rain Restaurant is located in a quaint building in Castries decorated with delicate filigree fretwork. It is one of the few remaining buildings that reflect the island's French heritage. It is a perfect lunch-time setting and serves great sandwiches, salads and fresh fruit drinks. The best tables are on the balcony overlooking Derek Walcott Square.

D's Restaurant

Vide Bouteille
Tel: 453-7931

D's Restaurant is situated beneath towering palm trees on the white sands of Choc Bay beach. The menu includes a selection of grilled fish or meat, as well as delicious home-made soups. There are daily lunch specials and a wide selection of salads. Specialities include sautéed chicken livers with sherry, and chicken *piccata* cooked with mint and yoghurt.

Opposite: Chicken tikka masala served with fragrant rice and traditional Indian breads is a favourite in Razmataz Restaurant. Below: Rain Restaurant is one of the few buildings in Castries that escaped the damage wreaked by two fires that devastated the city in the 1900s.

Spinnakers
Reduit Beach
Tel: 452-8491

Spinnakers is a popular restaurant located directly on Reduit Beach, adjacent to the St. Lucian Yacht Club. The theme is distinctly nautical with sails, surfboards suspended from the ceiling. You can have breakfast, lunch or dinner here. The daily specials are written up on a blackboard. Spinnakers is always a hub of activity and happy hour is extremely popular.

Burger Park
Rodney Bay
Tel: 452-0811

Burger Park is a great choice for a family meal. The burgers and chicken sandwiches are good value and vegetarian options are also available. The food is served quickly and you can eat outside beneath covered picnic tables. It is situated beside the island's only miniature golf course and a children's playground.

Shamrock's
Rodney Bay
Tel: 452-8724

Shamrock's is a lively bar with a casual, friendly atmosphere. It is a favourite haunt of locals and each evening there is either a live band or *karaoke*. The menu ranges from light snacks such as chicken wings to more hearty grilled steaks. There are also air hockey and pool tables, and mini television sets showing moments in sporting history.

The Fox Grove Inn
Mon Repos, Micoud
Tel: 455-3800

Take a scenic drive to the Fox Grove Inn, a country hotel that looks out over banana plantations across to the sparkling edge of Praslin Bay. It is an ideal spot to escape from the tourist track. If you are visiting for lunch or dinner you can use the pool, or take in a different view of the countryside on horseback, available by prior arrangement.

Key Largo
Rodney Bay
Tel: 452-0282
Fax: 452-9933

For a genuine taste of Italy, visit Key Largo for a pizza served straight from the traditional wood-burning brick oven. This large, bustling pizzeria is located just off the highway in Rodney Bay. Excellent pastas and salads are also served. Pizzas are not served between 3.00pm and 5.00pm in the afternoon while the oven is cleaned, but everything else on the menu is available. There is a good selection of Italian wine on offer.

Left: Local crab served with a zesty mango salsa. Below: St. Lucian restaurants offer a wide variety of excellent wines. Opposite: Restaurants often serve a unique mix of French gourmet and contemporary Caribbean cuisine.

The Lime
Rodney Bay
Tel: 452-0761

The Lime Restaurant is one of the "hot spots" on the island and is located in the centre of Rodney Bay. The bar is open to the street and is a favourite of locals, as well as holidaymakers. The Creole buffet lunch is good value, or choose from a selection of snacks, including a hearty roti or Jamaican jerk chicken. The Late Lime is a night-club that features a range of music from classical, reggae and calypso to country and jazz. There is a disco every Friday, and Saturday is jazz night.

The Snooty Agouti
Rodney Bay
Tel: 452-0321

The owners of Snooty Agouti have created a unique ambience in this cosy coffee-house style restaurant. Works of art by local and regional artists, as well as arts and crafts are on display, and many are available for sale. There is also a small book shop, a library, and internet access for visitors who want to maintain contact with the outside world! A huge cocktail list promises everything from strong rum punch to refreshing non-alcoholic fruit blends. The menu is

simple but fun, including baked potatoes and sandwiches with imaginative and tasty fillings. The restaurant also serves and sells a great selection of fresh coffee.

The Bistro
Rodney Bay
Tel: 452-9494

The Bistro is a lively waterfront restaurant overlooking the marina at Rodney Bay. Mooring is available for diners who choose to arrive by boat, and it is a perfect place to enjoy happy hour which often continues late into the evening. The menu is varied and well-priced, and features reliable favourites such as shepherd's pie or fresh lobster with garlic butter. There is also a great pasta selection. The wine list is varied and well-priced.

La Panache at Henry's Guest House
Cas en Bas Road
Tel: 450-0765

La Panache is a quirkily decorated guesthouse run by Henry and Roger. It nestles in the hillside along the road to Cas en Bas. On most Wednesdays, Henry cooks a Caribbean feast while Roger entertains the guests. This incredible repast is created from a combination of seasonal local produce and is a real taste of St. Lucia. Either chicken or fish are served with an selection of distinctive vegetable dishes of dashene, breadfruit, plantain, papaya and christophene. Always book at least twenty-four hours ahead to join this banquet. The meal is a set price plus drinks, and diners are welcome to bring their own wine if they wish.

the nitty gritty

planning your trip

how to get there; fare information; tour operators; when to go; what to pack; vaccination and immunisation; visa/immigration requirements; airline essentials & comfort

on arrival

airports; airport taxes

getting around

by air; by bus; by bus; by car

getting acclimatized

climate; business hours; courtesy & respect; electricity; media; money; post & couriers; religion; telephone; time, tipping; what to buy; what to wear

staying alive

health requirements; travel assistance and insurance; beat the heat; tropical diseases and cautions; personal security & safety; emergencies; hospitals; dentists; embassies and consultates

tourist information

St. Lucia tourist board
St. Lucia tourist offices overseas

Centuries of volcanic upheaval have created a spectacular dot of land in the middle of the Caribbean Sea. Lying between St. Vincent and Martinique, St. Lucia (pronounced LOO-sha) is 238 square miles (616 sq. km) of outstanding beauty, making it the second largest of the Windward Islands. Forest-covered volcanic plugs and mountains contrast with rushing rivers and lush valleys, while sheer cliffs and splendid beaches edge into the clear sea.

Many of the approximately one hundred and sixty thousand inhabitants are of African descent and speak a French patois. French influence is also obvious in the architecture, place names and the Catholic religion.

Not surprisingly, the beauties of St. Lucia have attracted filmmakers; the island provided spectacular location shooting for *Dr. Doolittle*, *Superman II*, *Firepower* and *Water* which starred Michael Caine.

"Stunning" is the word used most often to describe the many and varied attractions of St. Lucia. Spend days exploring the majestic rainforests or relaxing on the sparkling beaches. Try horse riding along the spectacular coastline or bird watching among the exotic trees and flowers. Then spend the nights dancing to the Caribbean beat, taking in a beach barbecue, or enjoying a quiet candlelit dinner at an elegant restaurant.

planning your trip

How To Get There

British Airways, Virgin Atlantic and BWIA are the only airlines to offer direct scheduled services from the UK; BWIA offers direct scheduled flights from Frankfurt and Zurich. Charter flights are also available. Most European flights fly via Antigua or Barbados, although Virgin's service from the UK is direct; Air France has a connection via Fort-de-France.

In North America, BWIA flies direct from New York and Miami; Air Canada from Toronto and Montreal; Air Jamaica from New York and Atlanta. American Eagle flies via its Puerto Rico hub in San Juan to gateway cities in the United States.

There are many competitively-priced connections from other Caribbean islands, flying with LIAT, American Eagle and Helenair.

Fare Information

In the UK:

British Airways ..0345-222111
Virgin Atlantic 01293-747747
Caledonian 01293-535353
BWIA.................0181-577-1100

In North America:

BWIA.................1-800-327-7401
American 1-800-433-7300
Air Canada 1-800-776-3000
Air Jamaica 1-800-523-5585

Tour Operators

The best bet is to put yourself in the hands of a knowledgeable travel agent, who can find the best offer to suit your requirements. Most trips are sold as packages, offering different destinations and resorts with the main flights included.

In the UK:

Airtours, Wavell House, Holcombe Road, Helmshore, Rossendale, Lancs BB4 4NB. Telephone: 01706-260000

Caribbean Connection, Concorde House, Forest Street, Chester CH1 1QR. Telephone: 01244-341131 Fax: 01244-310255.

Caribtours, 16, Fulham Road, London SW3 6SN. Telephone: 0171-581-3517; Fax: 0171-225-2491

Elegant Resorts, The Old Palace, Chester CH1 1RB. Telephone: 01244-329671; Fax: 01244-341084.

Thomas Cook Holidays, PO Box 36, Thorpe Wood, Cambridgeshire PE3 6SB. Telephone: 01733-332255.

Thomson Holidays, Reservations Number 0990-502399

In the USA:

American Express Vacations
Telephone toll free: 1 800-241-1700

Caribbean Concepts, Telephone: 516-496-9800; Fax 516-496-9880

GoGo Tours Telephone toll free: 1-800-526-0405

Travel Impressions Telephone toll free: 1-800-284-0044

When To Go

The dry season runs from November to May and the wet season from June to October. However, you can be sure that it will be always warm at any time of the year. Even in the rainy season, downpours are short and sharp and everything soon dries in the hot sun. Like much of the Caribbean, St. Lucia can be affected by hurricanes, either directly – Hurricane Debbie caused extensive damage, including the destruction of seventy per cent of the banana crop in 1994, or by high winds and rain from hurricanes that pass the Windward Islands at a distance. Officially, June to November is the season for tropical storms, but September is regarded as the month at greatest risk.

What to pack

Apart from beach wear (for the beach only!), the general dress code for the island is "elegantly casual", translating for women into soft, flowing attire for most restaurants and bars. Men should opt for casual trousers (not jeans) for smarter establishments. Between December and March, a lightweight jacket may be needed in the evening, especially if you take a sunset cruise or dine at a waterfront restaurant.

St Lucia boasts numerous ways to see the island – hiking through the rainforests, trekking to waterfalls or horseback riding along the rivers. If you plan to enjoy any of these activities a good pair of tennis shoes or closed walking shoes are a must; as are jeans for horseback riding. Keen bird-watchers should pack a set of binoculars.

If you are on regular medication, take supplies with you, as well as a copy of your regular prescription.

As far as photography goes, be self-sufficient. Bring a spare camera battery (or two), and plenty of film. Although film is available on the island, it is not cheap.

Remember to take a sunhat, sunglasses, high factor sunscreen, swimsuits, a basic first aid kit (include travel sickness pills, diarrhoea medication and rehydration salts) and plenty of insect repellent. If you wear contact lenses, remember to bring your regular cleaning solutions, as well as a spare set of lenses.

Vaccination and immunisation

There are no required vaccinations, but children's normal vaccinations should be up to date. The biggest plague, however, is the mosquito. and a good anti-mosquito cream containing citronella is highly recommended. There are many good ones to be found in the local drugstores.

Visa/Immigration Requirements

Valid passports – but no visas – are required by British citizens, as well as visitors from European Union or Commonwealth countries. If staying for less than six months, North

American visitors can enter with just an ID card, but must have a valid return air ticket with them on arrival.

Airline essentials and comfort

Always hand-carry your passport and visa, airline ticket, traveller's cheques, cash (including some EC dollars), credit cards, toiletry kit and plenty of reading material. It is also advisable to carry your driver's licence, itinerary, water and camera.

Make a photocopy of your passport and credit cards and keep them in a separate part of your luggage; be sure to know how to cancel your credit cards should they be stolen. It is sensible to always hand-carry jewellery and other valuables.

on arrival

Airports

Hewanorra International Airport, developed on the site of an American World War II base, is located in the south of the island, with the nearest main towns being Vieux Fort about a mile (1.6 km) to the south and Laborie some 3.5 miles (6 km) to the west. For most visitors staying at resorts in the north, this involves an hour-and-a-half drive along winding roads either by taxi or bus. Alternatively, you can pay approximately US$90 for a fifteen-minute air shuttle flight to Vigie by helicopter. However, these flights must be arranged in advance and all baggage is transported by vehicle a couple of hours later.

G. F. Charles Airport is located at Vigie, which is just five minutes from Castries and approximately twenty minutes from Rodney Bay. Marigot Bay is a twenty-minute drive (depending on traffic) through Castries, while Soufrière is one hour away along the west coast.

Airport taxes

At both of St. Lucia's airports, a departure tax of EC$54 per person must be paid for all destinations. It is advisable to have the exact amount in EC dollars so remember to keep enough cash at the end of your trip.

getting around

By air

If you are planning on doing any "island hopping", it is worth investing in one of three "hopper" tickets offered by LIAT (Tel: 758-452-3051), the largest carrier in the Eastern Caribbean, which flies in and out of Vigie Airport. Other inter-island flights are offered by Air Martinique (Tel: 758-452-2463), BWIA (Tel: 758-452-3778) and Helenair (Tel: 758-452-1958). Charters can be arranged through Helenair or Eagle Air Services (Tel: 758 452-1900).

Within the island, the only air travel is by helicopter. Contact St. Lucia Helicopters (Tel: 758 453-6950). There are helipads at both airports and a few resorts. (*See Sightseeing Spectacular, page 57*).

By bus

If you are looking for cheap and cheerful, go by bus. The island's buses are, for the most part, privately-owned minibuses with no fixed timetable. The drivers – who, it must be said, are not as "safety conscious" as those of authorised taxis – are licensed to operate on a specified route, which is denoted by number on the front of the bus. They run on all the main routes around the island. The northern service, departing from Darling Road, runs as late as 10pm (even longer on Friday nights), while the Bridge Street-based south service stops running in the late afternoon.

By car

If you like your independence and can negotiate pot holes, hire a car. Avis (Tel: 452-2202), National (Tel: 450-8721), Budget (Tel: 452-0233) and Drive-a-Matic (Tel: 452-0544) are customer-oriented and keep vehicles to a good standard. Most car hire companies have desks at the hotels, airports and in Castries. You have to be aged twenty five or over and pay for a temporary licence (EC$30), which car hire companies can usually arrange. If possible arrange the vehicle in advance as this is often cheaper, and you will have the peace of mind knowing a car is waiting for you. Jeeps can be rented from Cool Breeze Jeep Rental (Tel: 459-7729).

Motorbikes and scooters can be rented from Wayne's Motorcycle Centre in Vide Bouteille (Tel: 452-2059). Make sure you wear a helmet and are insured.

Driving in St. Lucia is on the left and signage is good, so it is not difficult to find your way around. The speed limit in Castries is 30 mph (48 kph), and you are unlikely to be able to go much faster out of town due to the state of the roads – not to mention some of the local drivers, who should be given a wide berth at all times!

It is a legal requirement to wear seat belts whilst driving. There are penalties for drinking and driving, as well as illegal parking.

Petrol stations are open Monday-Saturday from 6.30am-8pm; some are open on Sundays and holidays from 2-6pm. Petrol is expensive and must be paid for in cash.

By taxi

Certified taxi associations are based at both airports and all major hotels. The drivers have taken safety courses and are required to adhere to the government-regulated fares (a copy of this tariff is available at both airports). Always ensure you agree the fare before you get in the cab – and do not let anyone tell you there is an extra charge to have the air conditioning switched on! Be forewarned that rush hour traffic jams can be formidable when taxis can be hard to find.

There is also a water-taxi association operating out of Soufrière, which provides a relaxed way for guests to travel around the Soufrière area. All members are properly insured.

getting acclimatized

Climate

St. Lucia's climate is sub-tropical, with temperatures ranging from the mid-60s (18°C) to the mid-80s (29°C). The hottest time of the year is June through August, when it may get up to the mid-90s (35°C). However, the constant trade winds usually keep things comfortable. Keep in mind that evening temperatures drop to 10-15°C.

In the winter, the winds blow from the north east at about 8-16 knots; in summer from the south east at 8-12 knots – although when night falls the winds reverse as the land cools. Summers are, for the most part, hot and wet and the winters warm and dry. The rainy season runs from June through October, but there are never constant downpours. The coastal regions average 60 inches (150 cm) in annual rainfall, while the interior rainforests can get as much as 160 inches (400 cm). The sea temperature ranges from 75° (23°C) to 85° (29°C).

In summer, the sun rises at around 5.45am and sets around 7pm; in winter sunrise is about an hour later and sunset an hour earlier.

It is difficult to think of the Caribbean without thinking of hurricanes. The most likely month for these is September, although the "season" technically runs from the beginning of June through to the end of November. If you are unlucky enough to be around when one is on its way, follow local advice on when and where to take shelter and DO SO. Do not be foolish as they are potentially very dangerous. There is usually enough warning of an impending hurricane to give visitors the chance to leave before weather conditions deteriorate.

Business hours

Stores are generally open Monday-Friday from 8.30am-12.30pm and 1.30-4.30pm; Saturdays 8am-12.30pm. Stores at Gablewoods Shopping Mall are open Monday-Saturday from 9am-7pm. Most are closed on Sunday. The hours at the JQ Charles Mall in Rodney Bay are Monday to Saturday 9am-7pm with certain shops open on Sunday from 9am-1pm.

Banking hours are typically Monday-Thursday from 8am-3pm and Friday from 8am-5pm. They are closed on weekends and holidays. However, some banks have Saturday morning hours at their branches in and around the Rodney Bay Marina.

Post office hours are Monday-Friday from 8.30am-4.30pm and Saturday from 8am-12 noon.

Courtesy and respect

Politeness, respect and good manners are an integral part of Caribbean culture. St. Lucians practice this in everyday life, and naturally expect guests to do the same. A smile and warm greeting will go a long way.

When taking photographs of anybody or a small group of people, it is courteous to ask first. Many St. Lucians, especially the elderly, harbour mysterious ideas concerning photographs, believing that they can be used in *obeah* spells or will "steal their soul".

Electricity

St. Lucia is on 220/240, 50 cycles with square, three-pin plugs, so standard UK appliances can be used. American appliances will require adapters and transformers unless they are dual voltage.

Media

The major newspaper in St. Lucia is *The Voice*, which is published in English on Tuesdays, Thursdays and Saturdays. The *Mirror*, *The Weekend Voice*, *The Star*, *The Crusader* and *One Caribbean* are weekly papers. Overseas newspapers are available at some hotels, newsstands and shops. Sunshine Bookshop, the island's premier book sellers, stocks a wide selection of international newspapers and magazines. They are located in Gablewoods Mall, JQ Charles Mall and Pointe Seraphine.

Television offerings include those from the government-operated St. Lucia Broadcasting Corporation, the privately owned commercial Helen Television System (HTS) on Channel 4 or 5 VHF, and Cablevision.

Radio 100, a subsidiary of HTS, broadcasts entertainment and information ("Caribbean Adult Contemporary") twenty-four hours a day on FM frequencies 100.1 (Castries), 103.5 (the centre of the island) and 100.3 (south). Radio Caribbean International (RCI) broadcasts daily in Creole and English, and there is also the government-owned Radio St. Lucia.

Money

Like all the Windward and Leeward Islands, St. Lucia uses the Eastern Caribbean dollar (EC) as its currency, which is tied to the US dollar. In late 1999, the exchange rate was EC$2.70 to US$1 and EC$4.40 to UK£1. US dollars are also widely used in the tourist areas and it is therefore advisable to bring some with you. For many other currencies, such as the Deutsche Mark, rates are not even quoted.

Remember that when someone refers to a dollar, they are usually talking about an EC dollar. Make sure you clarify which currency you are talking about when you are negotiating for something!

It is better to exchange currency at a bank than a hotel, where you would get five to ten percent less on the exchange rate. Better rates are also given for cash than traveller's cheques. Remember that you need identification, such as your passport, when you change money. It is a good idea to keep all receipts of exchange transactions, which you may need to exchange extra local currency back into US dollars or UK pounds when you leave. But be sure to keep enough for your departure tax.

Banks

For hours of opening see Business Hours, page 152

Bank of Nova Scotia
William Peter Boulevard Tel: 452-2292

Barclays Bank PLC
Rodney Bay Marina, Tel: 452-9384
Bridge Street, Tel: 452-3306
Vieux Fort, Tel: 454-6255
Soufrière, Tel: 459-7255
Micoud, Tel: 454-4244

National Commercial Bank
John Compton Highway Tel: 452-2103
High Street, Tel: 452-5879
Pointe Seraphine, Tel: 452-4787
Vieux Fort, Tel: 454-7780
Gros Islet, Tel: 450-0928
Soufrière, Tel: 459-7450

Royal Bank of Canada
William Peter Boulevard Tel: 452-2245
Rodney Bay Marina, Tel: 452-9921

Credit Cards

All major credit cards are accepted at St. Lucia's shops and restaurants – in fact, they are generally preferred by businesses to traveller's cheques. Many credit cards will allow you to obtain local cash advances. All banks have ATM machines.

Post and couriers

St. Lucia's main post office is on Bridge Street in Castries, and is open Monday to Friday from 8.30am-4.30pm and Saturday 8am-12 noon. Poste restante is at the rear of the building; fax and photocopying facilities are upstairs. All villages and towns have sub-offices.

The St. Lucia Philatelic Bureau is located at the main Post Office, where collectors can buy the country's colourful commemorative stamps. There is a DHL office on Manoel Street in Castries and a Federal Express office at the North of Derek Walcott Square on Bourbon Street. There is a Quikpak service operated by LIAT at the airports.

Religion

The predominant religion in St. Lucia is Christian, with almost ninety per cent of the population being members of the Roman Catholic Church. Like other Caribbean islands with diverse ethnic strands, there are churches and centres for various evangelical and other creeds. Baptist, Pentecostal, Jewish, Anglican, Christian Science, Seventh Day Adventist and Methodist all have a presence in the community.

The largest Roman Catholic church is the Church of Christ in Castries. Tel: 758-452-4951. Most churches are in and around Castries, but there are others to be found in Soufrière, Vieux Fort and Gros Islet.

Telephone

The area code for St. Lucia is 1-758. To dial a St. Lucia number from overseas, first dial the international access code, then "1", and "758", followed by the St Lucia number.

For operator assistance, dial 0.

Direct-dial overseas and inter-island calls are possible from St. Lucia, and the connections are generally good, but expensive. It is wise to carry at least two long-distance calling cards – such as AT&T, MCI and Sprint. If the operator claims you cannot use a calling card, ask to be put through to an international operator, who can help. Unless you have money to burn, DON'T place a long-distance call at your hotel without using a calling card – hotels can add up to a 400 per cent surcharge!

The island's telephone system is operated by Cable and Wireless on Bridge Street in Castries, with a sub-office on New Dock Road in Vieux Fort and at Gablewoods Mall. Telex and fax facilities are available at all offices. Cable and Wireless phone cards can be purchased locally, and these work to phone abroad.

Cable and Wireless also provides a "Phone Home" service, which you can charge to major credit cards. To access this, dial 811.

Time

St, Lucia is in the Atlantic Standard Time Zone, five hours behind GMT four hours behind during daylight savings time). It is one hour ahead of North American Eastern Standard Time. If it is noon in St. Lucia, it will be 4pm in London, 11am in New York and 8am in Los Angeles.

Tipping

Most hotels and restaurants include a ten per cent service charge on the bill, unless otherwise stated. It is rarely left up to the individual, but you can leave a bit extra for exceptional service. Some all-inclusive hotels ask that no tips be given, but this will be stated in the information provided at check-in or at the hotel's orientation briefings. Taxi drivers will appreciate a ten per cent tip, while 75 US cents per bag is a good rule of thumb for porters and bellhops.

What to buy

Shopping in St. Lucia can lead to the discovery of some exceptional treasures. The island boasts some top-ranked artists, traditional crafts and good duty free facilities. There are good deals on batik fabrics and stylish cotton clothing, while paintings by some of the island's renowned artists are also popular. Local handicrafts can be excellent and range from pottery and wood carvings to hand-woven straw items and spice baskets. Think creatively when you look at local products – a coal pot might make a nice souvenir. Try some gentle negotiation as it is generally expected, especially at the markets. But do not push too hard, as that it is considered an insult.

Ti Bagay is a delightful gift shop filled with wonderful treasures to take home. They are located at the JQ Rodney Bay Shopping Mall and offer unusual gift items at great duty-free prices. These include beautiful gift items by renowned Caribbean artist Jill Walker; a great selection of Mexican pottery and glassware; and an excellent selection of the very best of St. Lucian arts and crafts. Remember to bring your airline ticket in order to take advantage of the duty-free prices. (Tel: 758-458 0399).

Don't forget about the two things synonymous with the Caribbean: music and rum. Check the local music shops and visit Bounty Rum's Roseau distillery south of Castries.

Do **NOT** buy coral; it is illegal to export many types of coral, particularly "black coral". Buying it also encourages the destruction of the precious coral reefs, which are already much diminished by pollution and the activities of mankind.

If you are interested in taking away some of the island flora, it is advisable to purchase it from **Garden Gate Flowers** at Hewanorra Airport to ensure the correct paperwork is completed. Plants exported to other countries must be accompanied by a "phyto-sanity certificate".

The largest and newest shopping mall is located in the heart of the Rodney Bay area. The ground floor features a spacious and well-stocked supermarket, along with a liquor store, delicatessan, post office, and banking facilities. The escalator leads to a number of interesting shops, some of which are duty-free. These include **Ti Bagay**, **Panache**, **Kokotok** and **Basic Blue**. There are two hairdressing salons, various places to eat and plenty of parking.

A good place to buy local books about the island is at **Sunshine Bookshop**. They are the island's best bookstore and have outlets at the Gablewoods Mall, the JQ Charles Mall in Rodney Bay and at Pointe Seraphine. Apart from an excellent selection of reading material ranging from current best sellers to educational titles, they also sell international newspapers and magazines. **Book Salon** is located on Jeremie Street.

If you are self-catering, there are plenty of bargains to be found at the colourful local markets. Try the fresh fish shop located in the market in downtown Castries. Fresh snapper, mahi-mahi, lobster and crayfish (when in season) are reasonably-priced and usually available. The **Fisherman's Cooperative Market** on the John Compton Highway at the entrance to Pointe Seraphine is also good for fresh fish. For a wide range of foodstuffs, try **JQ's Supermarket** near Vigie airport and at Rodney Bay, **Julian's Supermarket** at the Gablewoods Shopping Mall and Rodney Bay, or **Le Marché de France Supermarket** at Rodney Bay Marina. Fresh baked breads and pastries are available from the **Bread Basket** at Rodney Bay.

What to wear

As the weather is warm all-year round summer clothes are the rule – particularly cottons. However, you may need a wrap or sweater during the cooler winter evenings. The norm for men during the day is casual resort wear, unless one is attending any kind of official function, where smarter attire is required.

Swimwear should be reserved for the beach and do not wear it on the street or in town. The same applies to any skimpy clothing. In general, wear cool, comfortable, light-coloured clothing. Whilst you may see the odd occurrence of topless sunbathing, it is actually illegal in St. Lucia and it frowned upon by locals.

staying alive

Health Requirements

Although there are no required vaccinations, Hepatitis A and cholera vaccinations are also sometimes recommended. Latest information can be obtained by contacting the **Center for Disease Control** (CDC) Travellers Hotline in the United States (Tel: 404-332-4559; Fax: 404-332-4565).

Travel Assistance and Insurance

There is nothing worse than having a medical emergency – or falling ill – when you are on holiday. It is

therefore strongly recommended you take out sufficient travel insurance to cover medical treatment, as well as financial investment, luggage and contents replacement. Some policies may also reimburse you for delays due to weather or flight delays.

Check with your own insurance company to see if they can supply insurance either on a short-term or long-term basis. Travel agents can generally arrange something as well, but it pays to compare prices and shop around. Make sure you read the fine print and know what your exclusions are. And, importantly, once you have taken out the travel insurance, take a copy of the policy on holiday with you.

There are several well-known organizations, which supply medical policies and trip insurance packages to travellers. One of the largest is **International SOS Assistance**, who have a global referral network of some 2,500 medical professionals and assistance centres staffed around the clock, 365 days a year. They have many offices around the world, including Philadelphia (Tel: 215-244-1500 or 1-800-523-8930; Fax: 215-244-2227), London (Tel: 0181-744-0033), Madrid and Geneva. They also sell medical kits.

There are comprehensive schemes offered in the UK by **American Express** (Tel: 01444 239900); **Trailfinders** (Tel: 0171 938 3939) and **Jardine's** (Tel: 0161 228 3742). Similar companies in the US include

Travel Assistance International (TAI) in Washington, DC (Tel: 1-800-821-2828 or 202-331-1609; Fax: 202-331-1588); **TravMed** in Baltimore (Tel: 1-800-732-5309 or 410-296-5050; Fax: 410-825-7523) and **US Assist**, also in Washington (Tel: 202-537-7340).

Beat the Heat

It pays to remember that St. Lucia is in the "Tropical Zone" – the area that straddles the Equator. This means the sun is much stronger here than at home. Although the cool breezes will feel soothing as you lie on the beach, you are steadily baking – think lobster! If want to avoid ending up bearing a striking resemblance to the aforementioned crustacean – remember a few things:

Avoid the midday sun (even if you are an Englishman or a mad dog). Give yourself half-an-hour in the sun in the morning, and another half hour in the late afternoon. Clouds do NOT protect against UV rays. Look for a high SPF when choosing your sun lotion – and try to ensure it is water-resistant. If not, reapply each time you have been in for a swim.

Water reflects the sun's rays so if you are sitting beside the pool, or on the beach, you are experiencing a double dose of strong sun. The glare can also cause severe headaches.

Always wear strong sunglasses and a broad-brimmed hat. Don't be ashamed to cover up when you need to! If you are starting to turn pink today, then it is likely you will be as red as a beet tomorrow. Snorkellers, in particular, should beware of burnt backs: a long T-shirt – and even lightweight trousers if need be – will help avoid the problem.

You will recognize the onset of heat stroke by the following symptoms: your skin is red, hot and dry; your body temperature is high, you are confused mentally and you lose co-ordination. If this occurs you should seek medical help immediately.

Remedies for Sunburn

Calamine lotion applied to the skin – bring some with you, just in case

Liberally apply aloe, either the gel or sap straight from the leaf of the plant or commercial products

A mixture of two-thirds water and one-third vinegar, applied to the skin

Take aspirin regularly which will help reduce the inflammation.

Tropical Diseases & Cautions

Dengue fever: Yet another disease carried by that scourge of Mother Nature – the mosquito (in particular, *aedes aegypti*). Dengue fever can be hard to detect, because its symptoms are similar to flu: high fever, joint pain, headaches – but also an irritating rash several days later. There is no treatment for this disease so try to avoid getting bitten. Use repellents and cover up when the mosquitoes are most prolific at dawn and dusk. If you get

the disease, drink plenty of liquids, take pain killers *acetaminophen* (not aspirin) and rest. Unfortunately, about a year after having dengue fever, some people can develop hemorrhagic dengue: high fever, rapid pulse, measles-like spots and vomiting. If you get these symptoms, get yourself to a tropical diseases doctor immediately for treatment.

Venereal disease is prevalent in the Caribbean; including HIV, so remember the dangers of casual sex. Always check that properly sterilised or disposable needles are used should you require medical attention. St. Lucia's AIDS hotline is 758 452-7170.

Montezuma's Revenge

Well, no one wants to talk about it, but the sad fact is that many of us get it when we travel to an exotic destination: the dreaded diarrhoea. It is generally caused by viruses, bacteria or parasites contained in contaminated food or water. When in doubt about the condition of the water, used bottled and ensure it is sealed.

Make sure hot foods are cooked properly and cold foods have been kept cold. Peel fruit and vegetables before eating them. Avoid eating prepared food from roadside stands unless you are sure it has been kept at constant temperatures.

If you are still unlucky enough to be taken ill, there are a few things you

can do. If it is a serious case, seek medical attention immediately. Otherwise, take Pepto Bismol (*bismuth subsalicylate*), which slows down the process, but still lets it run its course. Avoid taking Imodium (*ioperamide*) unless you absolutely have to as it totally blocks up the digestive tract and locks in infections. Certainly do not take it for more than three days.

The best treatment is rest, plenty of fluids and salt replacement. The best antibiotic for bacterial types of travellers' diarrhoea is *Ciproflaxicin*. Take regular small portions of bland fluids – ginger ale, flat cola and salty chicken broth are all effective. Try to avoid getting dehydrated, which can be dangerous, especially for young children.

Nature's Nasties

Terrestrial beasts to be alert for include tarantulas, scorpions (although these are only found up in certain areas of the rainforest) and centipedes – none of which are deadly, but stings from the latter two are painful. Apply ice packs and a tourniquet if necessary to help relieve reactions.

More serious is the fer de lance – the island's only pit viper, which is found in a band across St. Lucia east from Dennery to west by Anse La Raye. The island's two main hospitals are usually equipped with the anti-venom, but the serum must be administered in hospital, since many people experience a severe allergic reaction to the treatment.

Hiking during the dry season – December through April – may also bring unpleasant encounters with chiggers, mites which live in the grass and pierce or burrow into the skin, leaving hard nodules and a small bumpy red rash at the point of entry. "Chigger Guard" is an excellent treatment; but even nail polish dabbed on the bites can be effective.

Some of the terrestrial flora can be equally unpleasant. Certain trees and plants should be admired only from a safe distance such as the **manchineel** tree, which grows in coastal areas. This is a medium-sized tree with bright green and glossy ovate leaves. Its green fruit resembles crab apples. Both the sap and the apples are toxic and can cause severe skin blistering. For this reason many are marked with a red band painted around the trunk. Do not take shelter under them when it rains, as the sap causes blisters when mixed with water. The Caribs originally used the sap to poison their arrow tips.

The prolific **oleander** is often used as a border for gardens and lawns; its usually pink flowers look much like the mountain laurel. The wood from this plant is extremely toxic and should not be burned – so if you have any impromptu

barbecues, avoid this willowy plant.

Marine menaces include young Portuguese men-of-war, which sometimes visit the Atlantic coast beaches. Generally light blue or pink in colour, tinged with purple, they appear to be tiny bubbles of plastic floating in the water, trailing a few thready tentacles. They can give nasty rope-like stings, which are painful but not dangerous. You can even get stung if you step on one that has been washed up on the beach, so tread with care. Tea tree oil applied directly to the affected area provides relief.

Personal Security & Safety

Common sense should prevail here and like anywhere else in the world, you must be careful.

Do not wear ostentatious jewellery, dress sensibly, lock up your valuables, carry only small amounts of cash, always lock your car doors, don't wander in deserted streets or on the beach late at night and keep hold of your purse at all times. Avoid threatening areas, such as ports, rowdy bars and red-light districts – particularly at night. Ask local advice on what other areas to avoid. If you do get robbed, don't try to be a hero just give them what they want and don't argue. Immediately contact your hotel security and local police.

If you are driving, don't stop if you are flagged down, no matter how callous that may seem. Don't make

something that is not your problem become your problem. And never pick up hitchhikers.

You will probably encounter street hawkers and peddlers on the beach. If you are not interested in what they are selling and don't want to be bothered by them, the best rule is a polite, but firm, "no thanks". On the street, it is easy: just keep on walking. On the beach it may not be that simple. If they persist or get increasingly obnoxious, remove yourself and find another spot. Beach constables are on patrol on some of the island's major beaches to deal with anybody who becomes an extreme nuisance.

Emergencies

For police, fire or ambulance, dial 999.

The police headquarters is in Bridge Street, Castries (Tel: 452-3854).

For air and sea rescue, telephone 452-2894 or 452-1182.

Hospitals

There are five hospitals on the island: **Victoria Hospital** on Hospital Road in Castries. Tel: 453-7059

Tapion Hospital, (the island's private hospital) on La Toc Road in Castries. Tel: 459 2000

St Jude's in Vieux Fort – a privately endowed hospital run by nuns Tel: 454-6041

Soufrière Tel: 459-7258

Dennery Tel: 453-3310

Dentists

There are a number of reliable dental surgeries on the island, including

Dr. K. Glace, Castries. Tel: 452 3840

Dr. A. Long, Castries. Tel: 452 6096

Rodney Bay Centre. Tel: 452 8621

In Vieux Fort contact Dr. M Marshall on Clarke Street. Tel: 454 5139

Pharmacies

For basic toiletries as well as medicines, try:

M&C's Drugstore on Bridge Street. Tel: 452-2811, ext. 216

M&C's at Gablewoods Shopping Mall. Tel: 451-7808

M&C's at the JQ Charles Mall in Rodney Bay. Tel:458-0178

Williams Pharmacy on Bridge Street in Castries. Tel: 452-2797

Clarke's Drugstore on Bridge Street. Tel: 452-2727

St. Lucia Health & Utility Services on Gros Islet Highway. Tel: 452-8271

Embassies & Consulates

British High Commission

N.I.S. Building, Waterfront Second Floor, P.O. Box 227, Castries
Tel: 452-2484/5/6
Fax: 453-1543
Open Mon-Fri 8.30am-12.30pm

French Embassy

Clarke Avenue,
P.O. Box 937, Vigie
Tel: 452-2462/5877
Fax: 452-7899
Open Mon-Tue 8am-2pm; Wed-Thurs 8am-5pm; Fri 8am-3pm

Federal Republic of Germany Consul

N.I.S. Building, Waterfront Second Floor, P.O. Box 233, Castries.
Tel: 452-3737
Fax: 450-0255
Open Mon-Fri 9am-12.30pm

Italian Vice Consulate

P.O. Box GM 848, Reduit Beach
Tel: 452-0933
Fax: 452-0869
Open Mon-Fri 1-4pm

Netherlands Consulate

M&C Building, P.O. Box 1020, Bridge Street, Castries
Tel: 452-3592
Fax: 452-3623
Open Mon-Fri 8am-4.30pm

Organisation of American States

Vigie, Castries
Tel: 452-4330
Fax: 452-4792
Open Mon-Fri 8.30am-12.30pm and 1.30-4.30pm

Embassy of the People's Republic of China

Cap Estate, Box GM 999
Tel: 452-0903
Fax: 452-9495

tourist information

The main tourism office in St. Lucia is in the Point Seraphine Shopping Complex, across the harbour from downtown Castries, where the cruise ships dock (P.O. Box 221; Tel: 452-4094; Fax: 453-1121). Other tourism offices are in Jeremie Street in Castries, at Vigie airport (Tel: 452-2595) and at the southern Hewanorra airport (Tel: 454-6644).

St. Lucia Tourist Offices overseas

London

421a Finchley Road, London N3 6HJ
Tel: 0171-431-3675
Fax: 0171-431-7920

Canada

8, King street East, Suite 700, Toronto, M5C 1B5
Tel: 416-362-4242
Fax: 416-362-7832

Germany

P.O. Box 1525, 61366 Friedrichsdorf
Tel: 6172-778013
Fax: 6172-778033

France

ANI, 53 rue François 1er, 7ième etage, Paris 75008
Tel: 74-203966
Fax: 74-230965

USA

4th Floor, 800 Second Avenue, New York, NY 10017
Tel: 212-867-2950/1-800-456-3984,
Fax: 212-867-2795

index